2 PETER

J. Vernon McGee

THOMAS NELSON
Since 1798

NASHVILLE   DALLAS   MEXICO CITY   RIO DE JANEIRO

Published in Nashville, Tennessee, by Thomas Nelson, Inc.

Scripture quotations are from the KING JAMES VERSION of the Bible.

Library of Congress Cataloging-in-Publication Data

McGee, J. Vernon (John Vernon), 1904–1988
   [Thru the Bible with J. Vernon McGee]
   Thru the Bible commentary series / J. Vernon McGee.
     p.   cm.
   Reprint. Originally published: Thru the Bible with J. Vernon McGee. 1975.
   Includes bibliographical references.
   ISBN 0-7852-1060-1 (TR)
   ISBN 0-7852-1118-7 (NRM)
   1. Bible—Commentaries. I. Title.
BS491.2.M37   1991
220.7′7—dc20   90–41340
ISBN: 978-0-7852-0864-8   CIP

Printed in the United States
HB 06.27.2017

CONTENTS

2 PETER

PREFACE

The radio broadcasts of the Thru the Bible Radio five-year program were transcribed, edited, and published first in single-volume paperbacks to accommodate the radio audience.

There has been a minimal amount of further editing for this publication. Therefore, these messages are not the word-for-word recording of the taped messages which went out over the air. The changes were necessary to accommodate a reading audience rather than a listening audience.

These are popular messages, prepared originally for a radio audience. They should not be considered a commentary on the entire Bible in any sense of that term. These messages are devoid of any attempt to present a theological or technical commentary on the Bible. Behind these messages is a great deal of research and study in order to interpret the Bible from a popular rather than from a scholarly (and too-often boring) viewpoint.

We have definitely and deliberately attempted "to put the cookies on the bottom shelf so that the kiddies could get them."

The fact that these messages have been translated into many languages for radio broadcasting and have been received with enthusiasm reveals the need for a simple teaching of the whole Bible for the masses of the world.

I am indebted to many people and to many sources for bringing this volume into existence. I should express my especial thanks to my secretary, Gertrude Cutler, who supervised the editorial work; to Dr. Elliott R. Cole, my associate, who handled all the detailed work with the publishers; and finally, to my wife Ruth for tenaciously encouraging me from the beginning to put my notes and messages into printed form.

Solomon wrote, ". . . of making many books there is no end; and much study is a weariness of the flesh" (Eccl. 12:12). On a sea of books that flood the marketplace, we launch this series of THRU THE BIBLE with the hope that it might draw many to the one Book, *The Bible*.

J. Vernon McGee

2 PETER

The Second Epistle of
PETER

INTRODUCTION

Simon Peter is the author of this epistle (see 2 Pet. 1:1). However, the Petrine authorship of this epistle has been challenged more than the authorship of any other book in the New Testament. Dr. W. G. Moorehead wrote years ago, "The Second Epistle of Peter comes to us with less historical support of its genuineness than any other book of the New Testament." Nevertheless, this challenge caused conservative scholars to give adequate attention to this epistle so that today it is well established that Peter wrote this letter.

In my teaching I spend very little time on issues of introduction, that is, on the authorship and other critical issues that have been raised concerning the different books of the Bible. I would ordinarily just pass over this because, to me, 2 Peter is a part of the Word of God and I think there is an abundance of evidence both internal and external. However, since I would not want to be accused of not even being familiar with the questions that have been raised concerning its authorship, we will face the facts on this issue.

The Second Epistle of Peter was a long time in being accepted by the church into the canon of Scripture. It was accepted at the council that met at Laodicea in A.D. 372 and then again at Carthage in A.D. 397, which was really the first time that the church had taken that kind of stand. Jerome accepted 2 Peter for the Vulgate version of the Scriptures, but it was not included in the Peshitta Syriac version. However, that version is not an acceptable one at all—there are other things about it that I am sure we would all reject—and, therefore, it is perfectly meaningless that 2 Peter was not included in it. Eusebius, one of the early church fathers, placed 2 Peter among the disputed books. Origen accepted it. Clement of Alexandria accepted it, and he wrote a commentary on it. Second Peter is quoted in the Apocalypse of Peter, which, of course, is not accepted as canonical. The Epistle of Jude apparently draws from 2 Peter and demonstrates that Jude was well acquainted with it. There are allusions and quotations from 2 Peter by some of the early church writers, including Aristides, Justin Martyr, Irenaeus, Ignatius, and Clement of Rome. You will also find that Martin Luther accepted it as genuine. Calvin actually doubted it but did not reject it. Erasmus did reject it.

That gives you some of the history of the background of this epistle, but the reasons that this epistle has been rejected by some cannot be substantiated. There is a great deal of internal evidence, especially certain autobiographical sections (see 2 Pet. 1:13–14; 1:16–18; and 3:1), which are to me absolutely conclusive that Simon Peter wrote this epistle.

Peter's second epistle was written about A.D. 66, shortly after his first epistle (see 2 Pet. 3:1) and a short while before his martyrdom (see 2 Pet. 1:13–14).

Second Peter is the swan song of Peter, just as 2 Timothy is the swan song of Paul. There are striking similarities between the two books. Both epistles put up a warning sign along the pilgrim pathway the church is traveling to identify the awful apostasy that was on the way at that time and which in our time has now arrived. What was then like a cloud the size of a man's hand today envelops the sky and produces a storm of hurricane proportions. Peter warns of heresy among teachers; Paul warns of heresy among the laity.

Both Peter and Paul speak in a joyful manner of their approaching deaths (see 2 Pet. 1:13–14; 2 Tim. 4:6–8). Paul said that he knew that the time of his departure had come. He had finished his course. He had been on the racetrack of life, and now he was leaving it. He had fought a good fight, and he had kept the faith. A crown of righteousness was laid up for him. You will find that same triumphant note here in 2 Peter as Peter also faced the prospect of death.

Both apostles anchor the church on the Scriptures, on the Word of

God, as the only defense against the coming storm of apostasy. It is no wonder that the enemy has attacked 2 Peter, because this is one of the finest shields that has been given to us to ward off the darts that the Wicked One is shooting at us today.

The similarities between 2 Peter and Paul's last epistle, 2 Timothy, also explain the sharp contrast between Peter's first and second letters. The subject of the second epistle has changed from that of the first; and the difference is, therefore, as great as that which exists between Paul's letters to the Romans and to Timothy.

In 2 Peter we see that apostasy is approaching, the storm is coming. How are we to prepare to meet it? There is only one way, Peter says, and that is through knowledge. Not only through faith in Christ, not only by believing in Him, but also to know Christ. "And this is life eternal," the Lord Jesus said, "that they might know thee the only true God, and Jesus Christ, whom thou hast sent" (John 17:3). We are to know Him and not only know about Him. I read the other day of an American preacher in Europe who is trying to start what he calls a Christian church without using the names of God and Christ. That is the most ridiculous thing that any man could possibly do. If he wants to start some kind of organization, let him go ahead and do it, but he cannot start anything that is Christian without Christ! To attempt to do that would be just like trying to make a peach pie without peaches or like trying to drive a car without any gasoline in the tank. If you are a Christian, you must know Christ. That means not to know about Him but to know Him—there is a great difference there.

The great subject of this epistle is going to be not only the apostasy but also that which will be our defense—knowledge. Where is this knowledge, and how does it come to us? Peter will say that the only way is through the Word of God, "a more sure word of prophecy," which he will talk about (2 Pet. 1:19).

You see, my friend, the Christian life is more than just a birth. It is a growth, and it is a development. The key to this entire epistle is the last verse: "But grow in grace, and in the knowledge of our Lord and Saviour Jesus Christ. To him be glory both now and for ever. Amen" (2 Pet. 3:18). Throughout the years of my ministry, I have often made the statement that I am not an obstetrician, I am a pediatrician. An obstetrician brings the little baby into the world. I thank the Lord that hundreds of people have been converted through listening to the Word of God, but actually I began my radio ministry of teaching the Word of God with the intention of helping believers to grow up in the faith. I am not an obstetrician bringing babies to birth, but a pediatrician whose job it is to give believers the milk of the Word and then to try to give them a porterhouse steak now and then. My friend, you will not be able to live for God in these days of apostasy unless you have a knowledge of the Word of God—and that is Peter's theme.

The theme of this second epistle is explained on the basis of the words which Peter uses here as contrasted to his first epistle. He does use certain words in both epistles. One word is *precious* which occurs twice in the first chapter. Peter, a great, big, rugged fisherman talked about things that are precious—that's a woman's word. The word *faith* is used again in this epistle and occurs twice in the first chapter. But the word that is especially characteristic of this second epistle is *knowledge*. It occurs sixteen times with cognate words. The epitome of the epistle is expressed in the injunction given in the final verse. This man Simon Peter went off the air saying, "But grow in grace, and in the knowledge of our Lord and Saviour Jesus Christ. To him be glory both now and for ever. Amen." This is what true Gnosticism is all about. The Gnostic heresy was that they had some little esoteric knowledge that no one else had. They had a form or formula, a rite or ritual, a secret order or password that you had to get on the inside in order to find out. Peter says that real knowledge is to know Jesus Christ.

OUTLINE

I. **Addition of Christian Graces Gives Assurance, Chapter 1:1–14**
"The full knowledge of God and of Jesus our Lord" is the foundation on which Christian character is built.

II. **Authority of the Scriptures Attested by Fulfilled Prophecy, Chapter 1:15–21**
Scriptures give light for obedience in dark days.

III. **Apostasy Brought in by False Teachers, Chapter 2**
Church should beware of false teachers and not false prophets.

IV. **Attitude Toward Return of the Lord—a Test of Apostates, Chapter 3:1–4**

V. **Agenda of God for the World, Chapter 3:5–13**
  A. Past World, 3:5–6
  B. Present World, 3:7–12
  C. Future World, 3:13

VI. **Admonition to Believers, Chapter 3:14–18**
Knowledge of God's program is an incentive to grow in the knowledge of our Lord and Savior Jesus Christ.

CHAPTER 1

THEME: Addition of Christian graces gives assurance; authority of the Scriptures attested by fulfilled prophecy

As I mentioned in the Introduction, this marvelous little epistle is the "swan song" of the apostle Peter; that is, it is his final word to believers before his death by crucifixion. He warns them of the apostasy which is coming, particularly of the heresy among teachers, and he seeks to anchor their faith on the Scriptures as the only defense against the coming storm.

In the first fourteen verses of this chapter, we shall see that the full "knowledge of God, and of Jesus our Lord" is the foundation on which Christian character is built.

ADDITION OF CHRISTIAN GRACES GIVES ASSURANCE

Simon Peter, a servant and an apostle of Jesus Christ, to them that have obtained like precious faith with us through the righteousness of God and our Saviour Jesus Christ [2 Pet. 1:1].

When we run across that little word *precious* in this very first verse we recognize it as Peter's word—he uses it several times in his first epistle, and he is the only writer of Scripture who uses it in this sense. It is like being able to recognize the handwriting on a letter. It is like seeing Simon Peter's signature when we see the word *precious* here.

"Simon Peter" is the way he begins this second letter. In his first epistle he simply used the name *Peter*. Simon was the name given to him at his birth, but *Peter*, meaning "rock," is the name our Lord Jesus gave to him. He uses both names in this epistle. Simon, the man of weakness, and Peter, the man of strength, the wishy-washy man and the rock-man—he has been both. But as he writes this epistle, we may be sure of one thing: he is the rock-man now, the man who is to be crucified for Christ.

"Simon Peter, a servant and an apostle." The word *servant* actually means "bond slave." He doesn't take an exalted position in the church. He refers to himself as a bond slave—also an apostle (that is his authority), but notice that he does not say *the* apostle, but *an* apostle; he was only one of them.

"To them that have obtained like precious faith with us." What he is saying here is quite wonderful. When he uses the word *faith*, I think he means the body of truth which we call the gospel. He is saying, "You have received it, and it is up to you what you do with it."

Those who hold what I call a hyper-Calvinistic viewpoint say that you have to be chosen before you can be saved and that God has to give you the faith to believe. Well, I'll go along with part of that, but I also insist that the reason some folk don't come to Christ is made clear for us in the Word of God. Notice 2 Corinthians 3:15–16: "But even unto this day, when Moses is read, the veil is upon their heart. Nevertheless when it shall turn to the Lord, the veil shall be taken away." When it says that "it" shall turn to the Lord, what is "it"? Well since the antecedent is the word *heart*, it is saying that when the heart shall turn to the Lord, the veil shall be taken away. My friend, if you are not a believer today, don't say it is because you have some *mental* reservations. The fact is that you have some *sinful* reservations. When the *heart* will turn to the Lord, then He will lift the veil. Anytime you are ready, God is ready, and He will save you. It is not God's will that any should perish. Today it is "whosoever will may come" and ". . . God so loved the world, that he gave his only begotten Son, that *whosoever* believeth in him should not perish, but have everlasting life" (John 3:16, italics mine). All He asks you to do is believe. He doesn't even ask you to clean up before you come to Him—but *He* will clean you up if you really mean business with Him.

They "have obtained like precious faith"—how? "Through the righteousness of God and our Saviour Jesus Christ." This is the righteousness which is made over to us when we trust Christ as Savior. You see, He not only subtracts our sin, He also adds to us His own righteousness. We are not like criminals who have been pardoned and turned loose; we have been given a standing before God, and that standing is in Christ—accepted in the beloved!

Grace and peace be multiplied unto you through the knowledge of God, and of Jesus our Lord [2 Pet. 1:2].

"Grace and peace be multiplied." Grace and peace are always in this order. We must first know the grace of God—that God has saved us, not through our merit, our character, or anything in us, but He has saved us because of our faith in Christ. Because He loved us enough to die for us on the Cross to pay the penalty of our sins, it is possible for Him to reach down and save us. Therefore, my friend, God saves you by grace. He saves you when you simply trust Christ, with no merit on your part. Once we experience God's grace, we can experience the peace of God also. This is what Paul is saying in his Epistle to the Romans: "Therefore being justifed by faith, we have peace with God through our Lord Jesus Christ" (Rom. 5:1).

Again let me say that we cannot consider Simon Peter an ignorant fisherman. As we see in his first epistle, he deals with more doctrine in a brief letter than any other New Testament writer. He takes up all controversial matters and handles them in a masterful way.

And he is a New Testament writer who uses arithmetic. He says, "Grace and peace be multiplied"—he is talking about multiplication. Paul didn't go into mathematics. He said that God is rich in grace and that the peace of God passes all understanding, but Simon Peter gets down to where the rubber meets the road. He takes out the multiplication table and says, "I hope grace and peace will be *multiplied* unto you." How wonderful this is.

He doesn't just leave it there. *How* will "grace and peace be multiplied unto you"? Will it be through some vision you have? Oh, no— "through the knowledge of God and of Jesus our Lord."

Now we are back to this word *knowledge*. We will be seeing it again and again in this epistle because of its importance. Paul also emphasizes this. Writing to the Philippians, he said, "That I may know him, and the power of his resurrection, and the fellowship of

his sufferings . . ." (Phil. 3:10)—oh, to know Him! Christianity is a
Person. We are not only to believe Him but also to know Him, my
friend. He is the living Savior who right at this moment is at God's
right hand.

It was the prophet Daniel who wrote, ". . . but the people that do
know their God shall be strong, and do exploits" (Dan. 11:32). My
friend, you are not going to do anything for God in the way of service
until you know Jesus Christ.

How does this knowledge come to you? Well, Peter won't leave
you in doubt; he won't let you hang in midair. When he gets through
with this epistle, you will know that the knowledge of Jesus Christ
comes through a knowledge of the Word of God, the sure Word of God.

To illustrate what Peter is meaning by the knowledge of God, let
me use the example of a well-known man who is no longer living.
Suppose someone were to ask me, "Do you know the late President
Eisenhower?" I would answer, "No, I never knew him."

"But you certainly heard about him."

"Yes."

"And you have seen him."

"Yes, I even saw him play golf once. I watched him hit the ball one
time, but then the Secret Service men glared at me; so I had to get out
of the territory. I did see him hit the ball, and the interesting thing is
that he didn't do much better than I do. But I cannot really say that I
knew him."

"If he were living today and were to walk right into your study, do
you think you would know him?"

"I think I would recognize him but I can't say that I would know
him. I never knew how he felt about things. I suppose that Mrs.
Eisenhower and his other loved ones knew him, but I never knew
him."

When Peter writes, "Grace and peace be multiplied unto you
through the knowledge of God, and of Jesus our Lord," he uses the
Greek word epignōsis, meaning "super knowledge." It is a knowledge
which comes by the Holy Spirit's taking the things of Christ and making them real to us. My friend, I believe that you can know Jesus
Christ better than you can know your closest loved one. And you can

tell Him things that you would not dare tell your closest loved one. The important thing is that to *know* Him is life eternal.

To know Him in this way, we first have to be born again, as Peter says, ". . . not of corruptible seed, but of incorruptible, by the word of God, which liveth and abideth for ever" (1 Pet. 1:23).

I remember hearing the late Dr. Herbert Bieber make the statement that after he was saved, he went to seminary to find out what had happened to him. That's good, and it reveals that you can *trust* Him and still not really *know* His Word.

> **According as his divine power hath given unto us all things that pertain unto life and godliness, through the knowledge of him that hath called us to glory and virtue [2 Pet. 1:3].**

"His divine power" has given to us all of the things which you and I need to live life to the full. I don't know about you, but I have always wanted to live it up. I don't mean that I have wanted to go out and paint the town red—you run out of paint when you attempt that sort of thing. But "his divine power hath given unto us all things that pertain unto *life* and *godliness*." Don't say that God has not made an arrangement for you to live for Him. He has made *every* arrangement for our life in Christ and our godliness of life for Him.

"Through the knowledge of him that hath called us to glory and virtue." Again we see this word *knowledge*. It is only through the knowledge of Christ that you can really learn to live down here and grow to be a more godly person. The only way in the world that you can become the kind of person with a fully developed personality is through knowing Jesus Christ. The knowledge of Him that "hath called us to glory" means to be like Christ.

"And virtue"—*virtue* means something more than we commonly think it means. I have spent a great deal of time with some of the words Peter uses because of their importance. The word *virtue* is not confined to chastity. We use it today when we refer to a woman being virtuous or morally chaste. Actually, *virtue* as Peter uses it has to do with excellence and courage. It means that you have the courage to excel in life. You don't have to live a little, mousy Mr. Milquetoast life and be a yes-man to everything that comes along. You can stand on your own two feet, state your position, and be counted for God. We certainly need that kind of "virtue" in this hour in which we are living, and the only way we can get it is through the knowledge of Christ. This is the formula Peter is giving to us here: "through the knowledge of him that hath called us to glory and virtue."

> **Whereby are given unto us exceeding great and precious promises: that by these ye might be partakers of the divine nature, having escaped the corruption that is in the world through lust [2 Pet. 1:4].**

Now why would Simon Peter call promises "precious"? In the first verse he talks about the precious faith that we have; now he talks about the precious promises that have been given to us. My friend, there have been given to you and me some glorious, wonderful promises here in the New Testament. Peter calls them "exceeding great and precious promises." For example: ". . . him that cometh to me I will in no wise cast out" (John 6:37); and "Come unto me, all ye that labour and are heavy laden, and I will give you rest" (Matt. 11:28)—the rest of redemption. "Take my yoke upon you, and learn of me; for I am meek and lowly in heart: and ye shall find rest unto your souls" (Matt. 11:29)—that's the rest of commitment of your heart and life to Christ. And another promise: "Jesus saith unto him, I am the way, the truth, and the life: no man cometh unto the Father, but by me" (John 14:6). Another wonderful promise is that of eternal life: "He that hath the Son hath life . . ." (1 John 5:12). "Being born again, not of corruptible seed, but of incorruptible, by the word of God, which liveth and abideth for ever" (1 Pet. 1:23). All these wonderful promises come through a knowledge of Jesus Christ and by faith in Him.

"That by these ye might be partakers of the *divine nature*," that is, that you might be a child of God! What a tremendous truth this is. This is overwhelming! When you are born again, you are given the nature of *God*, my friend. Don't let anybody deceive you into thinking that the Christian life is a little series of dos and don'ts—that if you do this and don't do that, you are living the Christian life. Oh, my friend, you are a partaker of the divine nature, the nature of God, and you *want* the things of God.

"Having escaped the corruption that is in the world through lust." This in itself is a tremendous statement. A little later Peter will speak of the make-believers who have escaped the pollutions of the world. What a difference there is between escaping the pollutions of the world and escaping the corruption of the world. The corruption of the world is that which is within us. The pollution of the world is that which is on the outside. At the time I am writing this, a great deal is being said about the antipollution programs. The feeling is that if we clean up the environment, it will produce nicer people. Well, it won't do a thing for the old nature, my friend.

Religious people go through an antipollution program on Sundays. They participate in a little ritual, a little washing, a little of this and a little of that. My friend, you can be religious to your fingertips and still be as corrupt as anyone can possibly be. Some folk that you see on Sunday don't look like the same folk when you see them on Monday. Why? Well, they have been through only an antipollution program on Sunday.

If you are going to escape the corruption of the world, you will have to have a new nature. You will need to be a partaker of the divine nature, having escaped the corruption that is in the world through lust.

However, although you have the nature of God through being born again, that doesn't mean that you have lost your old nature. There is a continuing conflict in the life of a believer between his new nature and his old nature. The best illustration of this in Scripture is that which our Lord gave us when He told the parable of the prodigal son (see Luke 15:11–32). Notice that the son *could* go to the far country because he still had an old nature. He *could* spend his money in riotous living, and he *could* even get down in the pigpen. But, you see, he was a partaker of the nature of his father, and his father didn't live in a pigpen. His father lived up there in a wonderful mansion. His father believed in godliness and cleanliness, and there was nourishing food on his table.

Now, that boy wouldn't have been his son if eventually he hadn't said, "I will arise and go to my father . . ." (Luke 15:18). He *had* to say it. You couldn't find a pig in the pigpen that would say that. Not one of those pigs went with him to his father's house. I read an article the other day by a man who raises pigs, and he claimed that they are clean little fellows. Well, he evidently has a breed of pigs which I know nothing about. However, we will see in 2 Peter 2:22 that a pig can get washed and cleaned up. Although he may become a tidy little fellow, even join a church, and become a deacon or a minister in the pulpit, he is still a pig and will eventually return to that pigpen. But the son is a partaker of the nature of his father, and he will eventually return to his father's house.

My friend, when you and I are children of God, we have the nature of God. Isn't that wonderful! We can understand God when He speaks through His Word and the Spirit of God makes it real to us.

But Peter doesn't stop with this, he goes on to say, "And beside this. . . ." I feel like saying to Simon Peter, "What in the world can you add to the promises of the Lord Jesus Christ and the fact of our being partakers of the divine nature?" I think that Simon Peter would answer, "Well, when you get that far, you have only started. There is a great deal beyond salvation."

Perhaps it will surprise you to know that there is something beyond salvation. You may recall that Paul said to Timothy that the Scriptures ". . . are able to make thee wise unto salvation . . ." (2 Tim. 3:15). Since Timothy was already saved, what does Paul mean by that? Well, salvation is in three tenses. Salvation is in the past tense: "I have been saved." It is also in the present tense: "I am being saved." And it is in the future tense: "I shall be saved"—"Beloved, now are we the sons of God, and it doth not yet appear what we shall be: but we know that, when he shall appear, we shall be like him; for we shall see him as he is" (1 John 3:2). I am not like the Lord Jesus now—I have not yet arrived—but I am in the process.

Now Peter is going to talk to us about Christians maturing. After a person is born again, he should not stay in the crib saying, "Da-da-da" the rest of his life. Nor should he need to be burped every so often. He should get to the place where he begins to grow up.

And beside this, giving all diligence, add to your faith virtue; and to virtue knowledge;

And to knowledge temperance; and to temperance patience; and to patience godliness;

And to godliness brotherly kindness; and to brotherly kindness charity [2 Pet. 1:5–7].

"And beside this, giving all diligence." The Christian life is a very serious business. However, we have made it sort of an extracurricular activity. The present-day thinking is that it is not something to be taken into the business world or the schoolroom or into social life. Rather, it is something sort of like your Sunday-go-to-meeting clothes which you wear only at certain times. However, Peter said that it is something to which we are to give "all *diligence*."

When Peter lists these graces which are to be added to our faith, they are not like a series of beads that you count off. Nor are they like a stack of dominoes which you stand on end in a long line, then when you push the first domino down, all the others fall down in a line. It is not like that at all. Neither is it like placing one brick upon another in building a structure. I know that Peter, in his first epistle, uses the figure of living stones being built up into a "spiritual house," but remember that all the stones were *living* stones.

Rather, the Christian life is a growth. This is the way Peter explains it in this epistle which closes with the tremendous statement, "Grow in grace, and in the knowledge of our Lord and Saviour Jesus Christ" (2 Pet. 3:18). A familiar illustration is that of a growing tree. You know the old proverb that great oaks from little acorns grow. (Sometimes we turn it around and say, "Great aches from little toe corns grow," but that is a different matter!) I am sure that you have watched a tree grow. I have a little redwood tree which was given to me by a dear lady who had previously lived in Oregon. It was just a little, bitty fellow in a can when she brought it to me. I didn't have a place for it at the time; so I just put it down in front of our living room window, intending to move it sometime. Well, the years went by, and that little six-inch tree is now almost as tall as I am and probably too big to move successfully. Likewise, the Christian life is to be a growth and a development.

Out in the woods two things are happening, things which are actually transfigurations. The vegetation that is living is growing, and the vegetation that is dead is decaying. Those are the two processes which are taking place out there. And one of those processes is taking place in your Christian life and mine.

If you are a child of God, you are to *grow*. And Peter lists the different attributes which are to characterize our growth. At the beginning, my little tree had very delicate needles, but they are different now— they are sturdy looking. And there should be growth and development like that in the Christian life.

Peter begins by saying, "Add to your faith virtue." The "faith" is saving faith, that which gave you your divine nature, that which gave you forgiveness of sins and made over to you the righteousness of Christ. Now you are to add to that, first of all, "virtue." Down through the centuries, some English words have changed their meaning, and *virtue* is one of them. *Virtus* to the Roman of the first century meant a great deal more than chastity. It characterized the very finest of Roman manhood: strength, valor, courage, and excellence. My friend, these same qualities should also characterize your life and mine. How the world needs believers who have the courage to stand for that which is right and to stand up and be counted for God in this day! Therefore Peter is saying, "Add to your faith courage."

"Add . . . to virtue [courage] knowledge." Here the Greek word for "knowledge" is *gnosis*, meaning "to know God in His salvation." It indicates growth. In verse 2 the word *knowledge* was the Greek word *epignōsis*, meaning "super knowledge." Paul, writing to the Colossian believers, said that he prayed that they might have this *epignōsis*, the super knowledge. The Gnostic heresy, which was abroad in that day, claimed to impart super knowledge by their secret rituals. However, "knowledge" for both Peter and Paul meant growth and development in the Christian life, and super knowledge was the goal as the Holy Spirit confirmed the Word of God to the heart.

Let me give you a personal example. When I was in college, I had doubts; in fact, I was very much of a skeptic and rather cynical at that time. Although I believed the Word of God, my faith was being torn to shreds in the liberal college I was attending. In fact, I said to one of the ministers who helped me a great deal that if I could not be convinced that the Bible was the Word of God, I would get out of the ministry. At that time I had faith, but it was a very weak faith. However, I can say dogmatically today that I not only believe the Bible is the Word of God, I *know* it is the Word of God. The Holy Spirit has confirmed it to me, and, and, friend, you cannot have a higher confirmation than when the Holy Spirit confirms the Word of God to your heart and life and makes it very real to you.

When young people ask me about a book which will show that the Bible is the Word of God, I have several in my library to suggest, but I haven't read one of those books in years. When I was their age, all I did read was books on apologetics. Well, I have long since passed that stage. My faith doesn't need that kind of propping up now. Some folk accuse me of being too dogmatic. No, I'm not too dogmatic; I am just sure and positive, that's all. If I didn't believe the Bible to be the Word of God, I wouldn't be teaching it. As I told that minister when I was in college, I would not go into the ministry unless I could stand in the pulpit with complete confidence in the Book which I was presenting.

Can you imagine a pilot taking two or three hundred people across the country in one of those great planes and saying, "Throw out the logbook and the maps and the charts. I don't have any confidence in them"? May I say to you, if you are sitting on such a plane, you are in trouble. But, of course, a man who is a commerical pilot believes in his logbook and his maps and charts. There is no need for you to get out of your seat and go to the cockpit and argue with him about them. He knows. He has information which has been confirmed to him—he has flown that route hundreds of times.

My friend, you can be sure of the Word of God, and as you study it and share it with others, the Spirit of God will confirm it to your heart, and you will experience growth in your spiritual life. This is what Peter had in mind when he said to add to your courage knowledge. You need courage to declare the Word of God. You are not apt to give out the knowledge that you have of Christ unless you have the courage to do it.

"Add . . . to knowledge temperance." That word *temperance* in our day refers to only one thing. A better word is *self-control*. As believers, we are to be self-controlled in every area of our lives.

"Add . . . to temperance [self-control] patience." Many folk have the wrong concept of what patience really is. They think it means sitting in a traffic jam on the freeway in the morning without worrying about getting to work. Well, that is not patience. It just gives you an excuse for being late to work. Patience is being able to endure when trials come. Patience is endurance. It is built upon knowledge and courage. Like a growing tree, a Christian should be developing courage, then knowledge, then self-control, and then endurance.

"Add . . . to patience godliness." *Godliness* is another word which has been lost in the shuffle. It means exactly what it says—to be like God. After you have been born into the family of God, you want to be like your Father—Godlike. It doesn't mean that you will be like God, but it does mean that you have that desire and aim in your life. I think of the words of a song we sing, "Oh, to be like Him. . . ." Well, it should be more than a song; it should be the desire of every individual who is a partaker of the divine nature. I believe there is a time in every boy's life when his dad is his hero and sometimes his idol. It is a terrible day when that idol falls from its pedestal, but it happens, and often the boy grows bitter. Well, we are children of God, and because of this, we want to be like our Father. And, my friend, He will never disappoint us. He is not only our hero, He is our God, the one we worship and praise. The word *godliness* has in it that very thought of praise and worship of God. It speaks of a dependence upon God and a life that is devoted to Him.

"Add . . . to godliness brotherly kindness." We can make that a stronger expression by translating it "love of the brethren." We are to love other believers. I receive many letters from those who listen to my Bible teaching on radio in which they say that they love me. And I can respond, "And I love you." If I met these folk personally, I am sure we would be more restrained, but certainly we should love the brethren. I have the opportunity of meeting with some very wonderful Christians—both laymen and preachers. Sometimes we eat lunch together; sometimes we play golf together; and sometimes we have a service together. It is a joy to have a sweet and loving relationship with the brethren.

"Add . . . to brotherly kindness charity." Again, the word *charity* means something entirely different in modern America from what it meant in 1611 when the King James Version was written. Since "brotherly kindness" is specifically for other believers, it is obvious that "charity" is to be directed to outsiders. I interpret it as meaning that we are to love the sinner as God loves him. God loved him enough to redeem him, but He hates his sin and will judge it unless he does turn to Christ. I take the position that loving a sinner does not mean getting down on his level and participating in his sin. Rather, we are to love him by bringing the gospel to him. My friend, the way we reveal our love to those outside the faith is to care enough to attempt to win them to Christ.

> **For if these things be in you, and abound, they make you that ye shall neither be barren nor unfruitful in the knowledge of our Lord Jesus Christ [2 Pet. 1:8].**

"If these things be in you." You see, Peter is not talking about the externalities of religion. He is not speaking of rituals or religion or liturgy. He is speaking of that which is inside the Christian. The reason he said that we have escaped the corruption of the world is because we are partakers of the divine nature. Corruption is inside the human heart. Later on he will say that the unsaved, that is, the apostates, escape the pollutions of the world (by going through a ceremony or acting religious), yet their hearts are not changed.

When he says, "If these *things* be in you"—what things? The things he has mentioned in the preceding verses: faith and courage and knowledge and self-control and patience and godliness and love of the brethren and love for the outsider. All of these things are to be within us.

"If these things be in you, and *abound*." Here he starts multiplying again. Peter is great with mathematics.

"They make you that ye shall neither be barren nor unfruitful." The word *barren* actually means "idle." This has to do with what we call the fruit of the Spirit. We cannot produce the fruit of the Spirit by sitting on the sidelines. While it is true that the fruit of the Spirit is the work of the Holy Spirit—that is, we cannot produce it by ourselves— we are to yield ourselves to Him, present our bodies definitely to Him, and draw from the Vine, the Lord Jesus Christ, the fruit of the Spirit. Again, the fruit is: faith, courage, knowledge, self-control, patience, godliness, love of the brethren, and love for the unsaved. He doesn't want us to be barren.

"Nor unfruitful" has to do with that which is, I believe, objective. Being barren has to do with that which is subjective, that which is internal. You have had, I am sure, the experience of meeting Christians who sound like sounding brass or a tinkling cymbal or an empty barrel. They are barren as far as the fruit of the Spirit is concerned. In contrast to this, we as believers are not to be unfruitful. Our lives are to be characterized by the fruit of the Spirit that Peter has been telling us about. My friend, does your life influence other people? Are you helping to get the Word of God out to folk who need it?

> **But he that lacketh these things is blind, and cannot see afar off, and hath forgotten that he was purged from his old sins [2 Pet. 1:9].**

Now Peter is touching on something which is very important to us; that is, sterility in the lives of many church members in our day. Their lack of enthusiasm will eventuate in their not being sure that they were ever really saved. Paul gives this admonition: "Watch ye, stand fast in the faith, quit you like men, be strong. Let all your things be done with charity" (1 Cor. 16:13–14). Then when he concluded his second letter to the Corinthians, he said, "Examine yourselves, whether ye be in the faith; prove your own selves. Know ye not your own selves, how that Jesus Christ is in you, except ye be reprobates?" (2 Cor. 13:5). This is a very strong statement. You are to *examine* yourself to make sure you are in the faith. If you have the idea that you can live a careless life and still be a Christian and *know* it, you are wrong. It is impossible. You may be a Christian, but you sure won't know it.

Many years ago a young preacher in Cannon Beach, Oregon, said to me one evening, "There are many Christians who believe in the security of the believer, but they do not have the assurance of their salvation." You see, the security of the believer is objective; the assurance of salvation is subjective. Peter has well stated it: "He that lacketh these things is blind, and cannot see afar off, and hath forgotten that he was purged from his old sins." He has forgotten that he has been saved.

> **Wherefore the rather, brethren, give diligence to make your calling and election sure: for if ye do these things, ye shall never fall [2 Pet. 1:10].**

"Give diligence to make your calling and election sure"—he means, of course, more sure. In other words, the security of the believer is objective; it is something that cannot be disturbed. However, your assurance can certainly be disturbed by the life you live. If your life is not lived in sincerity and truth, you are bound to lie on your bed at night and wonder if you really have been born again. While it is true that Christ has done everything necessary to save you and keep you saved, your Christian life to be meaningful is something that you have to work at.

I have been married for a long time, and I never have to lie awake at night and wonder whether or not I am married; but to make my marriage meaningful, I have to work at it, and I have been working at it for a long, long time.

Likewise in your Christian life, "make your calling and election more sure." That is, let it become subjective in your own heart—to know that you are a child of God.

"For if ye do these things ye shall never fall." I have talked with many Christians who have gotten into sin. It is very interesting to me that I have never yet talked to one who had the assurance of his salvation before he got into sin. You see, the person who lacks assurance lacks a solid foundation under him.

> **For so an entrance shall be ministered unto you abundantly into the everlasting kingdom of our Lord and Saviour Jesus Christ [2 Pet. 1:11].**

Notice that Peter will put an emphasis not upon the Rapture but upon the coming of Christ to establish His Kingdom upon this earth. Why? We find out in verse 14: "Knowing that shortly I must put off this my tabernacle, even as our Lord Jesus Christ hath shewed me." You see, Peter is one apostle who did not look forward to the Rapture. He knew he would never live to see the Rapture because the Lord Jesus had told him that he was to die a martyr's death. Therefore, he knew that shortly he must put off his tabernacle, that is, his body. This is a wonderful way to speak of death. Since Simon Peter knew that shortly he would move out of his body and into God's presence, he spoke of the everlasting kingdom of our Lord and Savior Jesus Christ, knowing that there would be no Rapture ahead for him.

> **Wherefore I will not be negligent to put you always in remembrance of these things, though ye know them, and be established in the present truth [2 Pet. 1:12].**

Knowing that he would not be with them very much longer, he felt called upon to stir up these saints to grow in grace, lest spiritual senility set in. There are Christians today—and I am sure you have met some of them—who are actually spiritually senile. They are tottering around, not seeming to have all of their faculties.

> **Yea, I think it meet, as long as I am in this tabernacle, to stir you up by putting you in remembrance [2 Pet. 1:13].**

"I think it meet"—that is, I think it fitting—"as long as I am in this tabernacle." Again he is speaking of his body as his tabernacle. As long as he had life, he was going to remind them of these important things.

> **Knowing that shortly I must put off this my tabernacle, even as our Lord Jesus Christ hath shewed me [2 Pet. 1:14].**

Here Peter is referring to what Jesus had told him that morning when He had prepared breakfast for them on the shore of the Sea of Galilee after His resurrection. He had said, "Verily, verily, I say unto thee, When thou wast young, thou girdedst thyself, and walkedst whither thou wouldest: but when thou shalt be old, thou shalt stretch forth thy hands, and another shall gird thee, and carry thee whither thou wouldest not." Then John comments, "This spake he, signifying by what death he should glorify God . . ." (John 21:18–19).

This passage in 2 Peter has been one of the most important sections in the entire Word of God. I have gone over it rather carefully so that you might know and understand what Peter is saying here.

You can see now why I have been calling this epistle Peter's swan song. It is, as it were, his deathbed statement. When a man is on his deathbed, he is apt to say something of importance even though he has not said anything of importance up to that time. If he has been a liar all of his life, the chances are that on his deathbed he will tell the truth.

It is interesting that the Word of God attaches some importance to deathbed statements. Let me illustrate this from the Old Testament.

Genesis 49 gives us a scene that is sad and rather dramatic. Jacob called his twelve sons to stand around his deathbed as he makes a prophecy concerning each one of those boys. Those prophecies have been literally fulfilled.

When Moses knew that he would not enter the Promised Land but would die on Mount Nebo in the land of Moab, he gathered the twelve tribes about him and blessed each of them before his death—very much as Jacob had done before him. It was a very important discourse that he gave to them at that time.

When Joshua was old and ready to depart from this life, he also gathered the tribes of Israel together and delivered to them his final charge. Then he challenged them to follow God and gave the testimony of his own life: " . . . As for me and my house, we will serve the LORD" (Josh. 24:15).

When David was about to die, he called Solomon to him. I don't believe that David would have chosen Solomon for his successor; he would have preferred Absalom, but Absalom had been slain. David said to Solomon, "I go the way of all the earth." (What a picture that is of death! I don't know who you are or where you are, but I can tell you the road on which you are traveling. You are going the way of all the earth, and that is to the cemetery. I realize that this doesn't sound very good, but all of us are on that route.) Then David charged Solomon with the responsibility of building the temple of God, and he exhorted all Israel to help him, for ". . . Solomon my son, whom alone God hath chosen, is yet young and tender, and the work is great: for the palace is not for man, but for the LORD God" (1 Chron. 29:1).

Then, in the New Testament when the Lord Jesus came into Jerusalem for that last Passover, He made it very clear to His own in His Upper Room Discourse that it was His last time with them while He was here in the flesh—before He would die and rise again in a glorified body. Oh, what tremendous truths He gave to them on that last evening!

The apostle Paul, as we have seen, gave his final epitaph in 2 Timothy. This is his swan song: "For I am now ready to be offered, and the time of my departure is at hand. I have fought a good fight, I have finished my course, I have kept the faith: Henceforth there is laid up for me a crown of righteousness, which the Lord, the righteous judge, shall give me at that day: and not to me only, but unto all them also that love his appearing" (2 Tim. 4:6-8).

Now Simon Peter says, "Knowing that shortly I must put off this my tabernacle." He knows that he has come to the end of his earthly life. Tradition tells us that he was crucified with his head down, and some folk have interpreted that to mean upside down. I personally don't think it means that. Rather, I believe the implication is that our Lord held his head up as He looked into the heavens, but Simon Peter felt himself to be unworthy to die in the same manner his Lord had died; so he died with his head down.

When Simon Peter said, "I must put off this my tabernacle," he was referring, of course, to his body. The word Peter used for "tabernacle" is the Greek skēnōma, which means "a tent or a dwelling place." Both Peter and Paul used that expression when referring to the body. Paul wrote, "For we know that if our earthly house of this tabernacle were dissolved, we have a building of God, an house not made with hands, eternal in the heavens" (2 Cor. 5:1). A tent is a pretty flimsy sort of thing, and if you don't believe that your little tent is flimsy, just step out on one of the freeways across this country, and you will find that your little tent will fold and you will silently slip away.

When we die, it is this little body that you and I live in that is put to sleep. The body sleeps in the dust of the earth. When God created Adam, He took his body out of the dirt. Man was created out of the earth. Our bodies contain fifteen or sixteen elements which can be found in the average soil today—that is the composition of the body. The body is put to sleep and returns to the dust of the earth. The Greek word that the Bible uses for "sleep" means "to lie down." In classical Greek it means "to go to bed."

A man who believes in "soul sleep" discussed this with me. I told him that "to sleep" means to go to bed and facetiously asked him to tell me which end of the soul he would stick under the cover and which end would go on the pillow. He hasn't been able to enlighten me yet, of course, because it is the *body* that sleeps, not the soul. It is the body that is like a tent. It is very feeble, and one of these days we are going to put it aside.

Paul also says, "We are confident, I say, and willing rather to be absent from the body, and to be present with the Lord" (2 Cor. 5:8). That is the way both Peter and Paul speak of death. This little tent we live in is put down into the grave. It goes to sleep, but the soul never dies. And, of course, the soul is never raised from the dead since it never dies. The word *resurrection* refers to the body. In the Greek it is *anastasis*, which means "to stand up," and obviously that refers to the body.

AUTHORITY OF THE SCRIPTURES ATTESTED BY FULFILLED PROPHECY

Moreover I will endeavour that ye may be able after my decease to have these things always in remembrance [2 Pet. 1:15].

"After my decease"—the word he uses means "exodus." He will just be moving out of his house, his tabernacle, down here; he will be putting it off as if it were a garment, and he will be making his exodus. Now the word *exodus* implies that death doesn't end it all. When the children of Israel went out of Egypt, the Egyptians said, "We are through with them. This ends it." But it didn't end it. Israel continued on in the wilderness and finally entered into the Promised Land, and Egypt doesn't seem to be through with them even to this good day! And for this man Peter, death was merely an exodus; it wasn't an end to it all.

"To have these things always in remembrance." Peter is saying that, in the light of his approaching death, he wants to bring before us certain things to keep in remembrance. And the thing he will really emphasize is the validity of the Word of God.

Now, there is a way of looking at the remainder of Peter's epistle that may be a little difficult to understand, but there are two forces in the world today. There is centrifugal force and centripetal force. A centrifugal force impels outward from a center. If you tie a ball on a string and swing it around your head, the ball will pull on the string, trying to get away from you. The centripetal force is just the opposite—it pulls toward a center or axis. Peter will deal with these two conflicting forces in relationship to the Word of God. There is a centrifugal force that impels outward from the world in which you and I live today, and there is centripetal force that pulls us into the world and away from the Word of God. My friend, the centrifugal force is the Word of God. It is the only thing that can pull us away from the world system. A letter from an alcoholic who began listening to our Bible teaching program by radio tells how the Word of God pulled him away from the bottle and from a worldly life and pulled him toward God.

Peter has already told us that we are to make our calling and election more sure, and he wants us to know that we have an authority on which we can depend. Somebody is going to raise the question, "How do you know that the Bible is really the Word of God?"

For we have not followed cunningly devised fables, when we made known unto you the power and coming

of our Lord Jesus Christ, but were eyewitnesses of his majesty [2 Pet. 1:16].

This is something that is very important for us to see.

"We have not followed cunningly devised fables." The Bible is not a pack of lies. The Bible is not a fairy story. The Bible is not a myth. The Bible is historical and factual. If you are sincere and want to give up your sins, God will make it real to you. If there is a veil over your eyes, it is not because you are mentally blind; it is because you do not want to give up your sins. When you and I are willing to do that, God will make the Bible real to us.

"But were eyewitnesses of his majesty." Now, I tell you, *that* is just a little disconcerting. When did Simon Peter see the power and coming of Jesus Christ?

He will make it clear that he is referring to the transfiguration of Jesus Christ.

For he received from God the Father honour and glory, when there came such a voice to him from the excellent glory, This is my beloved Son, in whom I am well pleased.

And this voice which came from heaven we heard, when we were with him in the holy mount [2 Pet. 1:17–18].

Obviously, Peter is referring to the Transfiguration. We need to understand the significance of this event. What did Jesus mean in Matthew 16:28? "Verily I say unto you, There be some standing here, which shall not taste of death, till they see the Son of man coming in his kingdom." This has led some people to claim that the Kingdom was well established at this point. (It is unfortunate that we have a chapter break at this point in Matthew's account—remember that in the original manuscripts there are no chapters.) The account continues: "And after six days Jesus taketh Peter, James, and John his brother, and bringeth them up into an high mountain apart, and was transfigured before them: and his face did shine as the sun, and his raiment was white as the light" (Matt. 17:1–2).

The transfiguration of Jesus Christ was a miniature picture of the Kingdom. Moses and Elijah appeared there with Christ. Moses represents the Law in the Old Testament. Elijah represents the prophets in the Old Testament. What were they discussing? They were discussing Christ's decease, His exodus, His passing from the room of this world into the presence of the Father. That is what they had written about in the Old Testament, and that is what they were talking about at the Transfiguration. Then there were the three disciples present to observe the Transfiguration. They represent the living saints. Moses and Elijah represent the dead saints of the Old Testament. The church was not yet in existence, but the three disciples who were there would constitute the beginning of that body of believers which is the church. They would be the apostles. So the Transfiguration gives us a miniature picture of the Kingdom.

Immediately after the Transfiguration, Jesus Christ and the disciples came down from the mount, and there they found a man with a demonized son. The other disciples could do nothing to help the boy. The observing people were jeering and ridiculing the disciples. That is a picture of the present day. The Kingdom is in abeyance. Jesus Christ is at the right hand of God, and all the Old and New Testament saints who have gone before are with Him. While down here on this earth we are living in a demonized world. If you doubt this, all you have to do to be convinced is to read your newspaper or watch your television newscast. The world is in a terrible mess. The church, which ought to have a message of hope and power for the world, is not helping this demonized world. As a result, the church is being ridiculed—and in one sense, rightly so—because the church is not about the Father's business as it should be.

Now Simon Peter has said that he was with the Lord Jesus on the Mount of Transfiguration. He was one of the eyewitnesses. Then he says this strange thing:

We have also a more sure word of prophecy; whereunto ye do well that ye take heed, as unto a light that shineth

in a dark place, until the day dawn, and the day star arise in your hearts [2 Pet. 1:19].

"We have also a more sure word of prophecy"—when he uses the word prophecy he doesn't necessarily mean the prediction of the future, although he includes that. He means the entire Word of God, because he speaks of the Scriptures as having been spoken by God. And the prophets, as he will make it clear in the next verse, were more than amanuenses who took dictation from God; rather, they expressed their own feelings and thoughts. Nevertheless, God was able to transmit His complete will and word through the men who wrote Scripture. This is the thing that makes it a miraculous Book. You see, the Word of God is not only divine; it is human, very human. It is like the Lord Jesus who was both God and man. The Bible is a God-book and a man-book. It deals with human life, right down where you and I live and move and have our being, yet it is God speaking to man in a language that is understandable to him.

A great many people think, "Oh, if only I could have been with Peter. If only I could have seen those things." Friend, you have something even better. You have the Word of God. It will speak directly to you if you will open your heart and allow it to speak. The Word of God is better than seeing and hearing.

"We have also a more sure word of prophecy"—rather "the word of prophecy is made more sure."

"A light that shineth in a dark place." The Word of God is a light, a lamp, a source of light, like the sun in the sky. It is a centrifugal force. As the sun gives out its light, throwing it out to the universe, so the Word of God sends out a light, a force, and a power. It is the only tangible supernatural thing that we have in this world today. The Word of God is the only physical miracle that we have from God in this hour in which we live.

It will be that until Jesus comes—"until the day dawn, and the day star arise in your hearts." Jesus is called the Bright and Morning Star in Revelation 22:16. Until He comes, His Word is the centrifugal force going throughout the world and drawing men away from the world system and putting them into the arms of God. What a picture we have here!

**Knowing this first, that no prophecy of the scripture is
of any private interpretation [2 Pet. 1:20].**

"Knowing this first." Simon Peter says that this is the first thing we
are to know. The word *knowing* is a knowledge that comes, not only
from the Word of God, not only from facts that can be ascertained—if
you have an honest heart, you can find out whether the facts in the
Bible are accurate or not—but these are things which you can know by
the Holy Spirit's making them real to you. As I have said before, I have
long since passed the stage when I wanted the Bible proved to me.
When I was in college, I did want the Bible proved to me; and if I
found that archaeology had dug up a spadeful of dirt somewhere that
proved a fact in the Bible, I would clap my hands like a little child and
shout, "Wonderful!" I don't do that anymore. I don't need a spadeful
of turned-up dirt to prove the Bible to me. The Spirit of God Himself
has made the Word of God real to my heart. I know there is a trans-
forming power in God's Word. I get letters from all over the world
which testify to that fact. There is power in the Word of God. This is
something that we can *know*, and the facts, confirmed by the Holy
Spirit, make it real to us.

"No prophecy of the scripture is of any private interpretation."
What Peter is saying here is that no portion of the Scripture is to be
interpreted apart from other references to the same subject. That is the
reason I put up such an objection to this idea of pulling out one little
verse of Scripture and building a doctrine on that one verse. If you
cannot get the whole body of Scripture to confirm your doctrine, then
you had better get a new doctrine, my friend.

I think a good illustration is the difference between riding in a
good, solid, four-wheeled wagon and on a unicycle. If you have ever
seen a person ride on that one wheel of a unicycle, you have noted that
he does a lot of twisting and turning and maneuvering around to stay
balanced on that one wheel. In the circus I once saw a man riding way
up high on a unicycle, and all of a sudden it went out from under him,
and he fell backwards. Believe me, he had a bad fall. And I thought,
*Oh, how many Christians are like that today. They base what they
believe on a single verse.* While it is wonderful to have one marvelous

verse of Scripture, if it tells a great truth, there will be at least two or three verses and usually a whole chapter on it somewhere in the Bible. Simon Peter is telling us that no passage of Scripture should be interpreted by itself. We need to confirm it with other Scriptures.

For the prophecy came not in old time by the will of man: but holy men of God spake as they were moved by the Holy Ghost [2 Pet. 1:21].

"For the prophecy came not in old time by the will of man." Obviously he is referring to Old Testament prophecy. It didn't come by the will of man. That is, Isaiah, for example, did not sit down saying, "I think I'll write a book because I need some money. I'll send it to the publisher, and he will send me an advance check, and then I'll get royalties for it." That is the reason some men write in our day, but that is not the way Isaiah did it. Listen to Peter: "For the prophecy came not in old time by the will of man." The prophecy of Isaiah was not something that Isaiah thought up.

"But holy men of God spake as they were moved by the Holy Ghost." "Holy men" does not mean that the writers were some superduper saints. It means holy in the sense of being set apart for this particular office. If you are a holy Christian, it means that you are set apart for Jesus Christ. *Holy* means "to be set apart."

"As they were moved by the Holy Ghost [Spirit]" is a delightful figure of speech. The Greek actually portrays the idea of a sailing vessel. The wind gets into those great sails, bellies them out, and moves the ship along. That is the way the Holy Spirit moved these men.

Here in California we have a yacht regatta each year. The yachts line up and start for Honolulu, Hawaii, to sail in around Diamond Head. (A man must be rich enough to own such a sailing yacht and to have the time to enter such a regatta.) Some time ago a doctor performed an operation on me one day, and the next day he was off sailing to Honolulu! When he got back, I was asking him about it. He told me that they have an extra sail which they put out when they get a good wind and that moves the boat right along. Well, this is exactly what Peter is saying in this verse of Scripture. These men who were set apart for the writing of the Scriptures were moved along by the Spirit of God.

Now let me remind you that this is Peter's swan song, and, like Paul in his swan song, he emphasizes the importance of the Word of God for the days of apostasy. Paul said, "All scripture is given by inspiration of God . . ." (2 Tim. 3:16), and Peter is saying that the writers of Scripture were moved along by the Holy Spirit. The thought is the same. It is wonderful to see how God could take each man and use him, without changing his style or interfering with his personality, to write His Word so that His message comes across. While Paul the apostle wrote eloquent Greek, Peter the apostle—since he was a fisherman and Greek was his second language—wrote Greek that was not quite as good. Yet God used both of these men to write exactly what He wanted to say—so much só that, if God spoke out of heaven today, He would have to repeat Himself, because He already has said all that He has to say to mankind. God has gotten His Word to us through men of different personalities and different skills. For this reason I call it a man-book and a God-book.

The written Word, like the Lord Jesus, the living Word, is both human and divine. The Lord Jesus could weep at a grave, but He could also raise the dead. He could sit down at a well because He was tired and thirsty, but He could also give the water of life to a poor sinner. He could go to sleep in a boat, but He could also still the storm. He was a man, but He was God also. And the Bible is both human and divine.

Simon Peter is telling us that we have "a more sure word of prophecy." He puts a sure rock under our feet. The Scriptures are something that we can have confidence in. No wonder the Word of God has been attacked more than anything else. If the enemy can get rid of the foundation, he knows that the building will come crashing down.

It is sheer nonsense for a preacher to stand at a pulpit and preach a sermon showing that he does not believe that the Bible is the Word of God. That, to my judgment, is as silly as the poor fellow in the insane asylum whom a visitor saw using a pickax on the foundation at the corner of the dormitory in an attempt to destroy the foundation. The visitor, wanting to be sympathetic, asked the man with the pickax, "What are you doing?"

"I'm digging away the foundation. Can't you see?"

"Yes, but don't you live in this building?"

"Of course I do, but I live upstairs."

For a preacher to discredit the Word of God is equally as insane. My friend, the Scriptures as we have them are a solid foundation on which to rest our faith.

The last time I was in Greece, I went again to the Acropolis in Athens and examined the Parthenon. I have examined it several times to make sure I am accurate in this statement: there are not two parallel lines in the place, nor is there a straight line. If you go to one end and look down, you will see that it comes up to a hump in the middle and then goes back down. The Greeks had learned that the human eye never sees anything straight which is straight. This, I believe, is the reason God says that we are to walk by faith and not by sight. We can't trust our own eyes nor our own ears, but we can rest upon the Word of God.

One of the greatest proofs that the Bible is indeed the Word is fulfilled prophecy. Over one-third of the Scripture was prophetic at the time it was first written. It is not to be treated as speculation or superstition because of the fact that a great deal of it has already been literally fulfilled. As someone has well said, "Prophecy is the mold into which history is poured." Fulfilled prophecy is, to me, one of the great proofs of the accuracy of Scripture. Peter has said, "We have also a more sure word of prophecy." Since one-fourth of prophecy has been fulfilled, this means that one-fourth of one-third of the Bible is fulfilled prophecy. Man cannot guess that accurately! There were three hundred thirty prophecies in the Old Testament concerning the first coming of Christ, and all of them were literally fulfilled. No human being can guess like that.

Let me give you an example. Suppose that right now I should make a prophecy that it is going to rain tomorrow. I'd have a 50 percent chance of being right, because it either will or it won't. But suppose I add to that the prediction that it would start raining tomorrow morning at nine o'clock. That would be another uncertain element. I am no mathematician, but it seems to me that this would reduce my chance of being right by another 50 percent. Now suppose that I not only say it is going to start raining at nine o'clock but also that it will stop raining at two o'clock. According to my figuring, that would bring down my chance of being correct to 12½ percent. And it would be a lot less than that if you figure it according to a twenty-four hour day. But suppose I add three hundred uncertain elements. I would not have a ghost of a chance of being accurate. Yet the Word of God hit it, my friend. It is accurate. The Bible has moved into the area of absolute impossibility, and that to me is absolute proof that it is the Word of God.

CHAPTER 2

THEME: Apostasy brought in by false teachers

APOSTASY BROUGHT IN BY FALSE TEACHERS

We have seen in the previous chapter the centrifugal force of the light of Jesus Christ that draws men away from the world and toward God. Now let's talk about the centripetal force; that is, the force that impels folk toward the world. It is a gravitational force, the pull of the world away from the Word of God.

The days that Peter is talking about in this chapter have now come upon us in our day.

> **But there were false prophets also among the people, even as there shall be false teachers among you, who privily shall bring in damnable heresies, even denying the Lord that bought them, and bring upon themselves swift destruction [2 Pet. 2:1].**

"But there were false prophets also among the people." Peter is writing to Jewish Christians, and "the people" he is talking about is Israel. "There were false prophets among the people of Israel," Peter says, "even as there shall be false teachers among you," that is, among believers, the church. There were false *prophets* in the Old Testament, but there are false *teachers* today. My friend, we do not need to beware of false prophets at all—that is not our problem. Any man who attempts to prophesy today will soon be proven a liar—there is no question about that.

During World War II, there was here in Pasadena, California, a man who predicted that the end of the world would come (if I remember correctly) on September 15, 1943. When that day came, newspaper reporters filled his yard and waited. Eventually he had to come out and say that he had misfigured it. He said that instead it would be September 15, 1944. The ministers in Pasadena who were meeting together in a prayer fellowship at that time were concerned about this man's prophecies and wanted to get a statement into the newspaper. I said to them, "Forget it. As far as I am concerned, on September 15, 1944, the man will be proven a liar." You know, the world didn't come to an end the next year either. What happened was that the newspaper reporters laughed at and ridiculed that man. Of course, it hurts the cause of Christ when anyone does that sort of thing. The man disappeared from this area, and I do not know where he is today.

We do not need to pay any attention to false prophets, but let me say this to you: You do need to check false teachers. You need to check all teachers, including the one whose book you are reading right now. I urge you to check what I say by the Word of God. Don't believe it because Vernon McGee says it. One man told me, "I teach a Sunday school class, and if anyone questions what I say, I tell them, 'Well, McGee says that.'" That is the wrong approach, my friend. The Word of God is what you are to rest upon.

I am amazed today how easily people are deceived by all kinds of teaching. People will fall for anything, and if you do not believe that, you ought to see the elaborate operations and headquarters of some of the cults which are located here in Southern California. You would be amazed, for it reveals that there are a great many people who have not heeded Peter's warning that false teachers are abroad. Instead, they listen to them and give them financial backing.

Some wag has put it like this:

> Little drops of water,
> Little grains of sand
> Make the mighty oceans
> And the beauteous land.
>
> So the daily pressures,
> Subtle though they be,
> Serve to shape the oddballs
> We call you and me.
>   "Little Drops of Water"
>   —Author unknown

We oddballs down here can really be taken in. Peter says, "Beware of false teachers."

In chapter 1 we saw that there were prophets of God in the Old Testament, and they prophesied 100 percent accurately. Peter now says, "But there were false prophets also among the people." There were not only true prophets but also false prophets among the people of Israel. One example of this is the time that Ahab and Jehoshaphat went out against the Syrians (see 1 Kings 22). They called in a bunch of the false prophets of Baal who urged Ahab and Jehoshaphat to go to battle. Jehoshaphat saw immediately that they were not getting a word from God, and he said, "Don't you have a true prophet of God here?" Ahab said, "Yes, but I keep him in prison because he never says anything good about me." Today a great many people don't like a preacher unless he says something nice about them all the time. Ahab was like that. This prophet of God, Micaiah, told him the truth, and Ahab didn't like that. But they brought Micaiah in, and he told Ahab, "If you go to battle, you will be slain." Ahab turned to Jehoshaphat and said, "See, he never says anything good about me!" It's too bad that Ahab didn't listen to him, because he was slain just as Micaiah said he would be. Micaiah was a true prophet of God, but there were also several hundred false prophets at that time.

"Even as there shall be false teachers among you." Dr Marvin R. Vincent, in his very fine *Word Studies in the New Testament*, says that this Greek word for "false teachers," *pseudo-didaskalos*, occurs only here in the New Testament. As we have said before, false teachers are the danger for the church today, and believe me, they are dangerous. What is a false teacher? A false teacher is one who knows the truth but deliberately lies for some purpose. It is either for some selfish reason, or he wants to please people, or he does it for money. There are many teachers like that today. They preach and say what people want them to say, although they know what the truth is—*that* is a false teacher.

There are other men who teach error *ignorantly*. Some of the great reformers of the past and some of the great post-apostolic church fathers believed and taught some things which we do not hold to today. We believe they were entirely in error on certain things. Those men were not false teachers. They believed they were teaching the truth, and that does not put them in the category of a false teacher. A false teacher knows what he is doing, and he does it deliberately.

"Even as there shall be"—Peter puts this period of apostasy out yonder in the future because it would be beyond his death. Jude also discusses this same subject of apostasy. The very fact that 2 Peter and Jude are so much alike has caused some of the critics to say that one copied from the other. Let me state it a little differently: When God wants to emphasize something, He says it twice. That is the reason that the Lord Jesus said, "*Verily, verily,* I say unto you." One "verily" is enough for Him, but when He says it twice, you had better sit up and listen. Therefore, this is something that God considers rather important. However, when Jude wrote, he said that there were *already* false teachers in the church. They came in quite early, by the way, and they have been in the church ever since.

I think we have in this first verse a good definition of false teachers: "Who privily shall bring in damnable heresies, even denying the Lord that bought them, and bring upon themselves swift destruction." "Damnable heresies" actually means *destructive* heresies. That which identifies these false teachers is that they deny Christ's work of redemption for them. They will appear in the church as members of the church; they will claim to be Christians, and they will work secretly under cover of hypocrisy.

Years ago I preached in a church which was a very fine, fundamental church where the people loved the Word of God. They called a pastor to that church whom they had questioned concerning whether he believed the Scriptures and whether he believed in their plenary, verbal inspiration. He had answered affirmatively to every question they asked. About two years later, I was in that city and found that the members of the church had scattered and were attending other churches. They told me that this man had absolutely misrepresented himself—that's what the kinder people said. Some said, "He *lied* to us." That's exactly what he had done. He had come into that church and actually been a hypocrite. He said one thing when he actually believed another.

Now false teachers have some true doctrine. There is not a cult that I know of which does not have some truth in it. That is the one thing that makes them very dangerous, ten thousand times more dangerous than if they were 100 percent in error. These teachers generally believe some things that are true. Our Lord said, "Beware of false prophets, which come to you in sheep's clothing, but inwardly they are ravening wolves" (Matt. 7:15). Paul warned the church at Ephesus, "For I know this, that after my departing shall grievous wolves enter in among you, not sparing the flock" (Acts 20:29). These wolves in sheep's clothing will absolutely destroy the flock and scatter them.

Our Lord made this clear when He gave us a picture of the condition of the Kingdom after His rejection, crucifixion, and resurrection. He would not establish His Kingdom on earth at that time, but He said that the Kingdom of Heaven would be like a sower sowing seed, like a mustard tree, and like leaven. Leaven has gotten into the bread today. The bread is the Word of God, and there is a lot of false teaching that goes out under the guise of being the Word of God.

> **And many shall follow their pernicious ways; by reason of whom the way of truth shall be evil spoken of [2 Pet. 2:2].**

"And many shall follow their pernicious ways." False followers will go after false teachers. I do not believe that God's elect can be permanently deceived. I believe that God permits a lot of the cults and "isms" in order to draw away from the true church that which is false, because those who are phony will go after that sort of thing. This is exactly what Paul said would take place: "For there must be also heresies among you, that they which are approved may be made manifest among you" (1 Cor. 11:19). In other words, the genuine child of God will not go in that direction. The Lord Jesus said, "My sheep hear My voice, and they will not follow a false shepherd" (see John 10:27). When you see people take out after one of these false teachers, they are either ignorantly deceived or they are deliberately deceived because that is what they believe and what they wanted to hear all the time.

> **And through covetousness shall they with feigned words make merchandise of you: whose judgment now**

of a long time lingereth not, and their damnation slumbereth not [2 Pet. 2:3].

"Feigned words"—the Greek word for "feigned" is *plastos*. Dr Joseph H. Thayer in his lexicon of the New Testament, says that *plastos* means "moulded, formed, as from clay, wax, stone." *Plastos*—does that sound like another word you've heard? We have a new word, a word that wasn't even in existence in Peter's day, yet in a way it was. *Plastic*—that's the word Peter uses here. I love that, because today you can buy a plastic pitcher, you can buy a plastic bucket, you can buy plastic dishes, you can buy plastic toys. You can buy almost anything in plastic because plastic can be molded into every possible shape.

May I say this, and I do want to say it kindly. There are also plastic preachers who can be molded and shaped by the people that they serve. They say what their congregations want to hear. They use plastic words. This is the reason that neo-orthodoxy, when it first appeared, deceived so many people. When I came to Pasadena many years ago to pastor a church here, another pastor came about the same time. He was an outstanding liberal who is pretty much known all over the world today. A member of his church attended my Bible class, and she said, "Oh, he is sound in the faith because he uses the same language that you do." I said, "Fine, but does he mean what I mean by it?" She was sure that he did. On Easter Sunday she called me and said, "Dr. McGee, you have been wrong in criticizing this man. He spoke of the *resurrection* of Jesus today." I asked her, "But did you go up afterward and ask him whether he believed that Jesus was raised *bodily* from the tomb?" She replied, "I'm sure that that is what he meant." I told her, "I'm sure that he didn't, but you ask him." The next day she called me, weeping, and said, "You know, he just ridiculed the idea of the bodily resurrection!" So I explained to her, "These fellows use our vocabulary, but they don't have our dictionary." In other words, they may say something, but the important thing is what they *mean* by what they say.

Peter tells us that false teachers will speak with feigned words, plastic words, words that are just molded words. They will fit their words to the people to whom they are speaking. They speak one thing to one crowd and then talk differently to another crowd. I know a man who can bring a fundamental message if he is in a fundamental group, but when he gets with a liberal group, he is just about as liberal as they are. He is a plastic preacher—you can pour him into any mold, and he will accommodate himself to it.

What is the motivation for these false teachers? I tell you, Simon Peter puts it right out in the open here: "And through covetousness." They do it because they are covetous. Covetousness is actually a form of idolatry. Sometimes it may be that they are covetous for a position, for a name, for popularity. Many of them are covetous of money.

I am not talking through my hat, my friend. I could give you example after example of the fact that there are many false teachers abroad today, but I will give you just one. I read a report in a very fine Christian publication which tells about a service held by a well known evangelist. They reported that the preacher introduced the evangelist, saying, "He is a man after my heart because he loves money just like I love it." As the evangelist spoke, he was forceful, he was dynamic, and he put on quite a show. For forty-five minutes he did not read one Scripture verse, not even his text. He partially quoted only three or four verses. He used the personal pronoun *I* 175 times. He referred to Jesus Christ only eleven times. There was laughter every two minutes during his message—he was quite a comedian. When the invitation was given, some twenty young people responded to the urgings of the evangelist and went forward. For what? They had not heard the gospel! This is something that is so prevalent in our country today. The average church member doesn't know the gospel when he hears it and does not recognize when he doesn't hear it. This is the tragedy of the hour in which we live. There are many false teachers abroad today.

I urge you to check on all Bible teachers and radio preachers that you listen to. Check on me. Am I teaching the Word of God? Examine the Word of God and *see* whether I am or not. And check yourself. Every child of God should examine himself to see whether or not he is in the faith.

"And through covetousness shall they with feigned words *make merchandise of you*." In other words, these false teachers are doing it for money. I personally resent all forms of promotion today. When I

return from a trip and sort through my accumulated mail, I will sometimes pitch letters into my wastebasket without even opening them.
The name of the organization is on the envelope, so I know who they
come from. I've been getting their letters for years, although I've never
contributed to those organizations. I don't know why they keep send-
ing out all that propaganda, but I do know this: they want to make
merchandise of me. It is my conviction that an organization ought to
appeal only to folk who are interested in their certain work. There are
many fine mission organizations, and there are many fine Christian
radio programs, but there are some that are nothing in the world but
promotion. One of the marks of a false teacher is that he is a promoter.
He is not interested in giving you the Word of God; he is not attempting to help you. He is attempting to get something from you, to make
merchandise of you. You are sort of a food trading stamp for him or a
luxury car for him.

"Whose judgment now of a long time lingereth not, and their damnation slumbereth not." This is something that has disturbed a great
many folk, including some in the Bible. For example, the psalmist
was disturbed that the wicked were getting by with their sin—or so he
thought. But then he said, "I went into the temple of the Lord." What
did he learn in the temple? All he learned in the temple was that God
is in charge and He will take care of the wicked (see Ps. 73).

The apostle Paul was mistreated again and again, and he resented
it. He would not let the authorities at Philippi release him from jail
and urge him to leave town secretly. He was a Roman citizen, and he
forced them to do it the right way. But Paul told us not to take vengeance. We are to turn our case over to God. The minute that we try to
get revenge we are taking God's place, because ". . . Vengeance is
mine; I will repay, saith the Lord" (Rom. 12:19). And if you try to get
revenge, you depart from your walk of faith. However, walking by
faith does not mean that you are a Mr. Milquetoast whom everyone
can push around and treat any way they please. Rather, it means that
you can say, "All right, brother, you have mistreated me, you have
done this to me, but I'm going to turn you over to the Lord." Paul
wrote, "Alexander the coppersmith did me much evil: the Lord reward him according to his works" (2 Tim. 4:14). "The Lord will take

care of him. I've turned him over to the Lord," Paul said concerning another brother who had mistreated him.

Peter assures us that God will also take care of these false teachers someday. When I heard of the death of a certain liberal not long ago, a man said to me, "Well, he's better off today than he was when he was in this life." Frankly, I'm not so sure about that because he must give account to God for his life. I would not want to have to go into the presence of God someday and have the Lord say to me, "Look, McGee, you came to a passage of Scripture that time, and you soft-pedaled it because you were afraid of criticism. You didn't teach it like it is written." God would hold me accountable for that. I will have to turn in a report to Him for my Bible-teaching ministry. May I say to you, you are going to have to turn in an account to God also.

It may look like God is slumbering; it may look like God is taking a nap. He may not seem to be doing very much about these false teachers, but He is, my friend. Habakkuk wondered whether God would do anything about the enemies of Israel, but he found out that in reality God was moving much too fast for him—He was not slumbering at all.

Now Peter will give us three examples of apostates in the past. His first example is of the angels who sinned (v. 4), and it is an example of how the *Devil* works. His second example is that of the world of Noah's day (v. 5), and it is the example of the *world*. The third example (v. 6) is the turning of the cities of Sodom and Gomorrah into ashes, and that is the example of the *flesh*. We have here the world, the flesh, and the Devil, but Peter puts the Devil first—the Devil, the world, and the flesh. These are the three enemies that you and I need to be aware of. John, the apostle of love, says, "*Love not* the world, neither the things that are in the world . . ." (1 John 2:15, italics mine). "The world" does not mean the beautiful flowers, the mountains, the trees, and the sea. It means the world system down here that is against God—*that* is what we are not to love.

Peter will talk first about the Devil and about the fact that God in the past has judged angels. The subject of angels and demons is highly debatable and very popular today. In fact, there is too much attention being given to it. Many books are being written about Satan and about demons and all that sort of thing. I suppose they have their place, but my feeling is that the positive side needs to be emphasized more. I have a message that I give, "Who is Antichrist?" and I always conclude that message by saying that I don't know much about Antichrist and I don't *want* to know much about him. The One I want to know is the Lord Jesus Christ. I cannot find anywhere where Paul or any other of the writers in Scripture say, "That I might know the Antichrist. . . ." But Paul does say, "That I may know him [the Lord Jesus], and the power of his resurrection, and the fellowship of his sufferings . . ." (Phil. 3:10). It is life eternal to know God, the Father, and the Son, the Lord Jesus, whom He has sent (see John 17:3). Scripture does not instruct us to know Antichrist or to know all about Satan. It is true that we are not to be ignorant of his devices. We need to beware of him, but we can pay too much attention to him.

For if God spared not the angels that sinned, but cast them down to hell, and delivered them into chains of darkness, to be reserved unto judgment [2 Pet. 2:4].

"For if God spared not the angels that sinned." Many commentators feel that this refers to the events of Genesis 6. I do not agree, because I do not believe that the "sons of God" mentioned there were angels. Genesis talks about the genealogy of *man*. It concerns that family which was leading to the coming of Christ, which would bring Him into the world. That line intermarried with the world, with the line of Cain, and brought about a generation who were so sinful that God finally brought the Flood upon them. That is what Genesis 6 is all about, and I do not think this verse here in 2 Peter has any reference to that at all.

Then what does this verse have reference to? I will have to do just a little bit of speculating, yet Scripture does give us some hazy glimpses of this. We find that Jude refers to these things also; the Book of Revelation gives us some inkling of it; and several of the prophets open this area to us just a little.

Man was sort of a Johnny-come-lately on this earth—we haven't been here too long. Before man was here on earth, apparently there was another creation. God had a program going long before man appeared on the scene, and there were many created intelligences. From among those angels, who were God's creation and who were His messengers, some rebelled against Him and apparently followed Satan. We are told in Revelation 12:7, "And there was war in heaven: Michael and his angels fought against the dragon; and the dragon fought and his angels." Back in the past there was a rebellion against God led by the creature we know today as Satan or the Devil. He has many names—he is the great deceiver; he is a liar from the beginning. This creature rebelled against God, and there followed with him a great company of angels.

Peter tells us that some of the angels who rebelled are already in chains, they are already incarcerated, but some of them have not yet been brought into that place of being inoperative. They are very active in the world today, and I believe they are the demons that we read about in the Word of God. I think we are seeing today a reappearance of the supernatural. I have considered giving a message on this subject of demons because so much that is false is being taught today. There is a reality in the supernatural world, and because a so-called miracle takes place does not mean that God did it. After all, Satan has a certain degree of power.

Therefore, this verse is a reference to that which took place before man was put on this earth, when there was a rebellion against God led by Satan.

"Cast them down to hell." The word for "hell" here is an unusual word which does not occur in very many places in Scripture. The Greek word is *tartarus*. The Greeks spoke of the lost being in *tartarus*. It is not hell as we think of it. Hell has not really been opened up to do business yet and will not be opened up until much later. The Devil is not in hell; he is abroad in God's creation. He goes into the presence of God, according to the Book of Job; and he is like a roaring lion, going up and down this earth, seeking whom he may devour, Peter told us in his first epistle. Although Satan is not in hell, certain of his angels have already been incarcerated.

"And delivered them into chains of darkness." The Greek word for "chains" is *seira*. Many believe it should be *seirōs*, for that is the word used in many of the better texts. *Seirōs* means "pits or caverns." The two words are very similar. Apparently these angels are in pits of darkness. People think of hell as being a place of fire, but I think it is a place of darkness. Darkness and fire just don't go together, because a fire makes light. Can you imagine being in darkness for eternity?

"To be reserved unto judgment." They have not yet been judged. The indictment has been made against them. God has declared them guilty, and they are waiting for the judgment to come.

And spared not the old world, but saved Noah the eighth person, a preacher of righteousness, bringing in the flood upon the world of the ungodly [2 Pet. 2:5].

"And spared not the old world." In chapter 3 Peter will talk about three worlds—the world that was, the world that is, and the world that is to come. God "spared not the old world," that is, the world before Noah.

"But saved Noah the eighth person, a preacher of righteousness." There were seven others with Noah. Noah, his three sons, their wives, and Noah's wife are the eight persons who came through the Flood.

"Bringing in the flood upon the world of the ungodly." The people were religious; they simply left the living and true God out of their religion. They were living as if God didn't exist at all. They were living in the flesh. It is a false idea today that you and I, in the flesh, have some good in us. Paul says, "I have discovered that in my flesh dwelleth no good thing" (see Rom. 7:18).

I read a report by Dr. Turnbull in his book, *Mountain People*. He made a study of a people called the Ik who have been discovered in Africa and who are absolutely living lower than animals. Dr. Turnbull reports that the children are cast off by the mother at the age of three and must provide for themselves or die. They find berries and bark and insects, and they scavenge around for what is left by wild animals. The stronger ones literally take food from the mouths of the elderly. The author said that it would be an insult to animals to call these people's behavior bestiality. Dr. Turnbull (who is a humanist and not a Christian) said that the Ik teach us that our much vaunted human values are not inherent in humanity at all, but are associated only with a particular form of survival called society, and that all, even society itself, are luxuries that can be dispensed with. In other words, man apart from God is nothing in the world but an animal, and it is an insult to an animal to say that. You see, it is God who gives values; it is God who gives moral standards, and none of them are inherent in us.

Noah lived in a day when there was rebellion against God, a day when the world had become lawless. Genesis tells us, "And God saw that the wickedness of man was great in the earth, and that every imagination of the thoughts of his heart was only evil continually" (Gen. 6:5). Violence was abroad in the earth in that day. God moved in with the judgment of the Flood and brought an end to that pre-Noachician world. It was a world that had become, with the exception of one man and his family, a totally godless world. God did well in bringing judgment at that particular time. You can well see that it would not have been long until the entire world would have been in such a condition that God would have had to judge it and there would have been salvation for no one after that. In His judgment God had in mind the future that was coming, and His judgment reveals His care and respect for the human life He had created.

Immediately after the Flood, in order to curtail lawlessness and crime, God gave to man this edict: "Whoso sheddeth man's blood, by man shall his blood be shed: for in the image of God made he man" (Gen. 9:6). It is nonsense today to argue against capital punishment by saying that the Bible says, "Thou shalt not murder." "Thou shalt not murder" has reference to an individual who harbors hatred in his heart and, expressing his own fleshly feelings in anger or hatred, he slays another human being. My friend, that's murder. But God has given to governments the authority to execute any man who takes another man's life. Why? Listen to me for just a moment: You do not show respect for human life by letting off a murderer who has destroyed another human being. You show respect and value for human life when you take the life of a murderer who fails to respect another human being but despises him by killing him for some selfish or sinful reason.

Today the pendulum of the clock of public opinion is over on the side of the criminal. The sympathy goes to him: "Oh, he's a human being. We don't want to take his life." But he took someone else's life! We have had many softhearted and softheaded judges in this land, and we are far from God and His Word. Lawlessness has become so bad that the people of California have voted to reinstate capital punishment. Yet it is almost impossible to enforce it because of the godless leaders we have today. They know not God. They know not God's plan and program. Instead of being put in prison, the criminals are running the streets today, and the honest citizens are in prison in their own homes. I was in a home recently in the East where there were half a dozen locks on one door because that lovely home had been broken into. Criminals and thieves are abroad today. Dignity and respect for human life are shown when they are locked up, my friend.

Our nation has more than three strikes against it. Not only are we a nation of alcoholics, but also of murderers and thieves. The situation is alarming. Why have we come to this point? When I was in college, they didn't teach morals because they said that was not the purpose of education. "After all," they said, "if you just educate little Willy, he will come out all right." Little Willy is sort of a cross between a piece of Dresden china and a hothouse orchid. You don't want to apply the board of education to the seat of knowledge for fear you might ruin his little "umph" and he won't be able to express himself like the little flower that he is! Well, little Willy is expressing himself today: he is a thief, he's a murderer, he's a homosexual. My friend, may I say to you, the Lord Jesus said that out of the human heart proceed the ugliest, nastiest things that are imaginable. We need discipline. The unsaved world must have discipline from a government. If it does not, that nation will be destroyed. God laid down this principle for governments following His judgment upon the world of Noah's day.

And turning the cities of Sodom and Gomorrha into ashes condemned them with an overthrow, making them an unsample unto those that after should live ungodly [2 Pet. 2:6].

You can read the record of this in Genesis, chapter 19. It was the flesh that God judged at Sodom and Gomorrah. The inhabitants were given over to sodomy. Homosexuality was approved of in Sodom, and it is approved of in the United States.

The flesh is an ugly thing. You and I have that old nature, and it is a nature which expresses itself in that which is ugly, that which is wicked, that which is nasty. You cannot make me believe that by making homosexuality lawful somehow or other you have added dignity to it. God has said that when men go down that low, He gives them up. You can take it or leave it, but that's what the Word of God says (see Rom. 1:18–32). The very fact that we have been lenient and have smiled on this type of thing has caused it to increase and grow within our land.

And delivered just Lot, vexed with the filthy conversation of the wicked:

(For that righteous man dwelling among them, in seeing and hearing, vexed his righteous soul from day to day with their unlawful deeds;) [2 Pet. 2:7–8].

"And delivered just Lot, vexed with the filthy conversation of the wicked." This word vexed doesn't seem to me to convey what Peter is really saying. Many people say that Peter does not use good Greek, and yet I have had to look up the meaning of more words that Peter uses than even the apostle Paul uses. The Greek word he uses here is kataponeō, which means, according to Trench, "to tire down with toil, to exhaust with labor." It means "to afflict, to oppress with evil," actually, "to torment." One of the methods that communism has used and which apparently is used now in many places is to break down an individual by constantly putting him under a bright light, constantly plaguing him with questions, by pulling out his fingernails, and by doing all manner of torture to him. This word has that idea in it. Lot vexed his soul in the city of Sodom. He was never happy there. He was tormented on the inside. It was torture for him to live in Sodom.

I never got that impression of Lot while reading the Book of Genesis, by the way. I'm glad for Peter's comment—otherwise I would be apt to say that Lot was not saved. By reading the story back in Genesis of when Lot went down to the city of Sodom, got into politics there, and lost most of his family, I would come to the conclusion that he was not saved. Even when you read what happened with the two single daughters who escaped with him, you might wish that they too had stayed back in Sodom. The point Peter is making is that God got Lot out of that city; He knows "how to deliver the godly."

We are told in verse 6 that all of this is given to us as an example. An example of what? I think that you and I are going to get two big surprises when we get to heaven. The number one surprise will be that there are not going to be some people in heaven who we were sure were going to make it. They really weren't genuine, although we thought they were. The second and bigger shock will be this: There are going to be some people in heaven who we never even suspected were real born-again children of God. They didn't have very much of a testimony down here. Lot is an example of this—I don't think this man had any testimony for God at all. When the angels came and said that the cities of Sodom and Gomorrah would be destroyed, Lot went around to his sons-in-law and said, "I've got word from God that He is going to destroy this city. He's going to judge it. Let's leave!" The record says, "But he seemed as one that mocked." I suppose that they said, "We don't believe you, old man. The kind of life you've been living down here doesn't reveal to us that you have had very much faith and confidence in God." If I had only Genesis to read, I would have come to the conclusion that Lot didn't make it to heaven, that he was not a saved man. But Peter says, "He delivered just Lot"—and that does not mean only Lot, because his two daughters went with him, and his wife, although she didn't get too far away. Lot was called "just" because he was justified in God's sight.

"And delivered just Lot, vexed with the filthy conversation [manner of life] of the wicked." He didn't go for the way they lived; he hated it. He was a just man, which means that he was justified before God because he trusted God as Abraham did, although he didn't lead a life like Abraham, one that was a testimony to the world. Lot stands on the page of Scripture as a saint of God who was justified because of his faith, but his life denied everything he believed and he never had a moment's peace down here.

"For that righteous man dwelling among them, in seeing and hearing." Just think of the filth that that man had to listen to! Very candidly, I do not believe that a child of God can continually engage in filthy conversation. Filthy conversation will lead to filthy action.

God said to this man, "Lot, you will have to get out of the city. I cannot destroy it with you in it." You see, in the meantime there was a man named Abraham who was not criticizing Lot but was praying for him. That is a good lesson for many of us. There is a preacher, a friend of mine, who criticizes everything and everybody. One day he was criticizing an outstanding Bible teacher whom I respect and know that God has mightily used. I said to my friend, looking him right straight in the eye, "Have you ever prayed for him?" He turned red and said he hadn't. I said, "Instead of criticizing him, why don't you pray for him? If you think he is wrong, pray for him."

Abraham prayed for the city of Sodom. He wanted his nephew Lot to be spared. Abraham asked God to spare the city for the sake of fifty righteous people. He finally got it down to ten righteous people, and then he stopped praying because he was afraid that Lot was not really a child of God. But Lot was, and God got him out. God said, "I cannot destroy the city until you get out."

Mrs. Lot left with him, but she looked back and was turned into a pillar of salt. That may sound strange. Why should she be turned into a pillar of salt just because she looked back? My friend, it's what turning and looking back means. Why did she look back? It is obvious that, although she walked out of Sodom, she had left her heart back there. She was intertwined in everything that took place in that town—she belonged to the country club, the Shakespeare club, and every other kind of club. Perhaps the bridge club was having a meeting that afternoon and she really wanted to go. I think she plagued Lot, saying, "Why do we have to leave like this?" Another reason she turned and looked back was because she didn't believe God would destroy the city. Well, He did destroy the city, and He turned her into a pillar of salt.

The greatest lesson for us in these verses is that God's rescue of Lot from Sodom prefigures the rapture of the church. May I say to you, the rapture of the church will take place before the Great Tribulation period, before the judgment comes, because God will not let any of His saints go through it. Even those who are like Lot, the weakest saints, will be taken out. Lot made it, and if you have trusted Christ as your Savior, you can be sure that you will be going out too. This is a marvelous example of the fact that the church will not go through the Great Tribulation period. They have been justified by faith in Christ, and this man Lot was justified also.

The Lord knoweth how to deliver the godly out of temptations, and to reserve the unjust unto the day of judgment to be punished [2 Pet. 2:9].

To those who believe that the church is going through the Great Tribulation period, I would like to say that God knows how to deliver His own. You may not know how, but God knows how. He also knows how "to reserve the unjust unto the day of judgment to be punished." God knows the difference between the godly and the unjust—I don't. The wheat and tares are growing together today, and He said, "Let them alone. Let them both grow together." I'm not worried about the tares today, although I must confess that I wish there weren't so many of them. But wheat and tares are growing—the Word of God is getting out in this glorious day in which we live. One of these days He will make the separation, when He takes His own out of the world and when the lost will be brought before the Great White Throne for judgment.

But chiefly them that walk after the flesh in the lust of uncleanness, and despise government. Presumptuous are they, self-willed, they are not afraid to speak evil of dignities [2 Pet. 2:10].

"But chiefly them that walk after the flesh in the lust of uncleanness." This is a strong statement that Peter makes here. It actually means in the *defilements*—the defilements of uncleanness. This is a picture of those who are really lower than animals. They are those who delight in that which is vulgar, vile, and vicious. They relish that type of thing.

"And despise government." Many commentators say that this refers to government here on earth. I have reason to believe, since this word occurs so few times in the Word of God, that it really means "dominion." The same word *kuriotēs* is translated "dominion" in verse 8 of Jude and "lordship" in the first chapter of Ephesians. In Ephesians it has to do with spiritual governments. In other words, they despise that which is spiritual, that which God has ordained above us: the angels and the way God is running His universe. They are the ones who ask God to damn everything under the sun. They are not pleased with anything.

Not only that, Peter says, "Presumptuous are they." That means they are daring. They are daredevils. They don't mind blaspheming. It makes them feel expansive and big to use such language.

"Self-willed"—that is, they are going to do their own thing.

"They are not afraid to speak evil of dignities." The word for "dignities" is actually *glories*. They speak evil of that which is sacred, that which is holy. Isn't it interesting that men take God's name in vain? They don't take the city's name in vain or their boss's name in vain or the name of some person they hate. But they take God's name in vain. They are not afraid to speak evil of dignities, of glories, of this order that God has established in His universe.

> **Whereas angels, which are greater in power and might, bring not railing accusation against them before the Lord [2 Pet. 2:11].**

The false teachers are lifted up with pride, and they do something that angels don't dare to do. In the little Epistle of Jude, we find that Jude gives a specific instance of this when Michael the archangel was disputing with Satan about the body of Moses. You see, the Devil didn't want Moses to appear later in the Promised Land (at the transfiguration of Jesus), and so there was some dispute. God buried the body of

Moses. And Jude tells us that Michael would not bring a railing accusation against the Devil, but he simply said, ". . . the Lord rebuke thee" (Jude 9). This is a spirit that we need to manifest today, a spirit of humility, in the sense that we turn all of this over to God. It is pride that causes us to speak as we do. When I hear someone, sometimes even a Christian, talking about the Devil, ridiculing him and calling him names, I have to say that Michael the archangel wouldn't do that, and if Michael, exalted as he is, wouldn't do it, a little man down here on earth needs to be very careful.

But these, as natural brute beasts, made to be taken and destroyed, speak evil of the things that they understand not; and shall utterly perish in their own corruption [2 Pet. 2:12].

"But these, as natural brute beasts." These apostates are like wild animals. We hear a great deal today about man descending from an animal, but both the Old and New Testaments make it very clear that man is capable of living *lower* than the animals. He's not descended from anything. He's right down with them, if you please, and lives like an animal. Peter will give an illustration of this a little later on in this chapter.

They are natural wild animals, "made to be taken and destroyed" just like an animal is taken. They've descended to that low plane and have reached the place where they are hopeless and helpless.

They "speak evil of the things that they understand not." This that Peter says of false teachers can also be applied to many others. Something that has amazed me ever since I became a Christian is how smart some men who are not Christians can be and yet they do not at all understand the Word of God. There have been many brilliant men in the past who had no knowledge of what the Word of God is about. Let me give you an example.

William Wilberforce, a member of the British Parliament, was an alcoholic and lived a very fast life until he was converted. He wanted his friend, Edmund Burke, to hear one of the great preachers of Scotland, and when they were up in Scotland, he took Burke to hear this preacher. Afterward, he was interested to get Burke's reaction to the sermon. His reaction was very simple, and it revealed something. Burke said, "That man is a brilliant orator, but *what* was he talking about?" Edmund Burke, one of the great English statesmen, when he heard a gospel message, said,"I don't even know what he is talking about!"

Also I was very much interested to read recently something about a great denomination in this country, a church that down through the years has preached justification by faith. They made a survey and found that 40 percent of their members believe they are saved by their own works. How tragic it is to see that people do not understand the gospel! Many who have been hearing it year in and year out do not understand it at all.

"And shall utterly perish in their own corruption." Earlier Peter talked about the fact that the child of God has escaped the corruption of the world—but these have not escaped the corruption. Some of them have escaped the pollutions of the world. In other words, there are many lost sinners who say, "I wouldn't do the things that this low-down individual is doing"—and he wouldn't. He has escaped the *pollutions*, but he has not escaped the *corruptions*. On the outside he is religious; he goes through forms; he does certain works, but his heart is not right with God at all. He has a corrupt heart, and he has done nothing whatsoever about that.

And shall receive the reward of unrighteousness, as they that count it pleasure to riot in the day time. Spots they are and blemishes, sporting themselves with their own deceivings while they feast with you [2 Pet. 2:13].

In verses 13–14 we see in the description of apostates the utter corruption of the human heart. When a man thinks wrong, he is going to act wrong—you just cannot escape that fact. There are a great many people who say, "This is my life. I can live it as I please." It is well known that we have men today in government who are definitely immoral. They have affairs with women who are not their wives. We know that most of them drink, and many of them drink to excess. They say,

"This is my business. My private life is my business." My friend, their private lives are not their business if they are representing this government and representing my country. If they want to lead that kind of life, they ought to get out of government, because they are hurting their country and they are hurting us. We want men in government who are sober, men who are honest, men who are moral men. This is what is desperately needed today.

Having eyes full of adultery, and that cannot cease from sin; beguiling unstable souls: an heart they have exercised with covetous practices; cursed children [2 Pet. 2:14].

My, this is harsh language that Peter uses in speaking of false teachers! They are guilty of all of these immoral excesses, and don't kid yourself that God does not intend to judge them someday.

Which have forsaken the right way, and are gone astray, following the way of Balaam the son of Bosor, who loved the wages of unrighteousness [2 Pet. 2:15].

Balaam is mentioned three times in the closing books of the New Testament. In 2 Peter it is the *way* of Balaam. In Jude it is the *error* of Balaam. And it is the *doctrine* of Balaam in the Book of Revelation. Each one is different. What is "the way of Balaam"? Peter says he is "the son of Bosor who loved the wages of unrighteousness." Balaam knew that he should not go and prophesy against Israel, but he loved the price that was being offered to him. Therefore, "the way of Balaam" is the covetousness of one who does religious work for personal profit.

But was rebuked for his iniquity: the dumb ass speaking with man's voice forbad the madness of the prophet [2 Pet. 2:16].

Peter says that Balaam was mad to go and that the jackass he was riding spoke to him. Some wag has said that in the old days it was a miracle when a jackass spoke and now in our day it is a miracle when one of them keeps quiet! This jackass spoke to Balaam and rebuked him because of his covetousness.

My friend, I believe that you can judge the religious racketeer by his standard of living. A friend of mine heard me make the statement that people should check up on radio broadcasters and see what kind of homes they live in and what cars they drive. He thought I was wrong to have made a statement like that, but he decided to check up on one man. He found that man living in a very costly home with two Cadillacs parked in front and an expensive swimming pool behind it. My friend had also heard about certain other excesses in that man's life, and so he decided that he was supporting the wrong broadcaster. "The way of Balaam"—covetousness. This is one of the ways a false religious teacher can be identified, and God will judge him for it.

These are wells without water, clouds that are carried with a tempest; to whom the mist of darkness is reserved for ever [2 Pet. 2:17].

As a boy I lived in West Texas. We left there in the third year of a three-year drought. I can remember when we would go into the fields and chop cotton—believe me, in those days cotton didn't grow well in that country even if there was rain. But sometimes late in the afternoon big thunderheads, big clouds, would gather overhead, and there would be lightning. We'd think, *My, we are going to have rain*—but we didn't have rain. How dry it was! Many people are following false teachers who are like that. They are "wells without water." They are like clouds, beautiful clouds. Oh, how tremendous it is to see and hear these folk. They are very impressive, but there is no water in the well, and there is no rain in the clouds. People are thirsting today for the Word of God, and yet it is not being given to them.

For when they speak great swelling words of vanity, they allure through the lusts of the flesh, through much wantonness, those that were clean escaped from them who live in error [2 Pet. 2:18].

"For when they speak great swelling words of vanity." These false teachers use beautiful, flowery language. They soar to the heights oratorically, speaking in basso profundo voice.

"They allure through the lusts of the flesh, through much wantonness." It is a religion that appeals to the eye, a religion that appeals to the ear, a religion that appeals even to the nose. One preacher said to me, "I always have my church sprayed on Sunday morning." He wants it to smell good. Don't misunderstand me—I think the place ought to look nice; the music ought to be good music, and I don't mind a fragrant smell, but those things are not to be depended upon. They are the lusts, the desires, of the flesh. But Peter is accusing the false teachers of more than this. "Through much wantonness" refers to lewdness, sexual excesses.

This man Simon Peter is really being sarcastic now—

> **While they promise them liberty, they themselves are the servants of corruption: for of whom a man is overcome, of the same is he brought in bondage [2 Pet. 2:19].**

"While they promise them liberty, they themselves are the servants of corruption." Some habit has these false teachers enslaved, and yet they are promising liberty to others!

"For of whom a man is overcome of the same is he brought in bondage." This is the picture that we have before us: they promise liberty, but they don't really know what it is themselves.

> **For if after they have escaped the pollutions of the world through the knowledge of the Lord and Saviour Jesus Christ, they are again entangled therein, and overcome, the latter end is worse with them than the beginning [2 Pet. 2:20].**

These apostates have a head knowledge of Christ. They know the truth but have no love of the truth. They reject what they once professed and become enslaved in some sort of corruption.

And, my friend, I hear many folk say, "Oh, I am very religious. I belong to a certain church. We don't believe the Bible is really the Word of God, but we talk a lot about love and brotherhood. We have a beautiful church and a lovely service that makes us feel good." Such people have escaped the pollutions of the world. They are horrified when they read of crime and violence in the newspaper. You see, they have escaped the pollutions of the world but not the corruptions.

"Through the knowledge of the Lord and Saviour Jesus Christ." It is not that they haven't heard the gospel. They *have* heard the gospel. One man told me, "I listen to your Bible broadcast nearly every day." But he had to admit that he didn't believe anything; he even doubted that there was a God. That man knows the gospel. When someone asked me, "Why don't you present the gospel to him sometime when you're playing golf?" I told him, "He's heard me present the gospel over a hundred times. There is no need of saying any more." Peter says "They are again entangled therein, and overcome, the latter end is worse with them than the beginning."

In this chapter Peter has dealt very definitely with the apostasy that was coming into the church through false teachers who were creeping in and teaching false doctrines, teaching that which is contrary to the Word of God. Peter says that they pervert the truth of God, and they do it for their own advantage. These false teachers exalt themselves instead of exalting Christ. They do not use the Word of God except for a few little proof texts that more or less clothe their teaching with a pious halo. They use big words which are counterfeit words. They try to impress people that they are very intellectual, and they are interested in making money. They claim that they can change people. I know that I will get into trouble by saying this, but I think you ought to examine very carefully anyone who claims to have a supernatural power to heal or to perform miracles. Another thing that sometimes identifies a false teacher is that he is living secretly in lust and sin. You and I cannot fight these false teachers; I'm not attempting to fight them; I'm just trying to expose them. But one day *God* is going to expose them, and He is going to judge them.

For it had been better for them not to have known the way of righteousness, than, after they have known it, to

turn from the holy commandment delivered unto them [2 Pet. 2:21].

Now Peter concludes all this by saying that it actually would have been better for them not to have known the way of righteousness than, having known it, to then turn from the gospel.

I have done something in my ministry which has not been original with me at all. I heard the late Dr. A.C. Gaebelein say this, and it was so effective and so true that I have used it on many occasions. I will sometimes conclude a message by saying, "Friends, if you came in here today unsaved and you walk out of here unsaved, I am the worst enemy that you have ever had, because you have heard the gospel and you can never go into the presence of God and tell Him that you have never heard the gospel. You have heard it, and it will be worse for you when God pronounces judgment than for any heathen in the darkest part of the earth today."

But it is happened unto them according to the true proverb, The dog is turned to his own vomit again; and the sow that was washed to her wallowing in the mire [2 Pet. 2:22].

Peter speaks of these false teachers, using the term *dog*. To the Jewish mind there was nothing lower than a dog, by the way. "The dog is turned to his own vomit again." Peter draws from Proverbs 26:11 to show that they will return to their true, natural, unchanged condition.

"And the sow that was washed to her wallowing in the mire." It is Simon Peter who gives us the parable of the prodigal pig. You may never have heard the parable of the prodigal pig, but here it is. It is, of course, based on the parable of the prodigal son, which is one of the greatest parables the Lord Jesus ever gave (see Luke 15:11–32).

There are those who say that you cannot preach the gospel from the parable of the prodigal son. However, the first time that I ever went forward in a meeting was under a brush arbor in southern Oklahoma in a little place called Springer. It's not much of a place today, I'm told, and it certainly wasn't in that day. I went forward and knelt down, and all I can remember of that night is that the preacher preached on the prodigal son. I can remember the figures of speech that he used. He took the prodigal son through all the nightclubs and places of sin. That night all the saints sinned vicariously through the preacher's message. Believe me, it was a very effective message. I'm confident that others got saved that night, but nobody took the time to explain to me about the gospel. I didn't really understand it, and my life afterward revealed that I wasn't saved, but my heart was certainly open for it.

Actually, the story of the prodigal son is not how a sinner becomes a son but how a son becomes a sinner. The account, as recorded in Luke 15, is a familiar story. You remember that there was a father who had two boys. One of the boys, the younger one, wanted to take off for the far country. Dr. Streeter calls this the sin of propinquity. That is a big word, but it simply means that the things near at hand are not so attractive but that the faraway places have an allurement, an enchantment. I think the chief allurement of sin is its mystery. The old bromide that grass is greener on the other side of the fence is the story of this boy.

So the boy ran away and soon was living it up. When he had plenty of money, the fair-weather friends were with him, but they soon faded away. He ended up having to go out and get a job working for a man who raised pigs. When the Lord Jesus mentioned that, both the publicans and Pharisees winced, because a Jewish boy could have sunk no lower than that. He hit bottom. In effect, he was on drugs, involved in sexual immorality, and all that type of thing. This boy was down in the pigpen.

Again, let's understand what the parable is primarily teaching. It is not showing how a sinner gets saved, but it reveals the heart of the father who will not only save a sinner but will take back a son who sins. Someone asked the late Dr. Harry Rimmer, "Suppose the boy had died in the pigpen? What then?" Dr. Rimmer said, "Well, if he had died in the pigpen, there is one thing for sure, he would not have been a dead pig. He was a son." He was a son when he left home; he was a son when he got to the far country; he was a son while he was living in sin; and he was a son in the pigpen. And because he was a son, he made a statement one day, a statement that no pig could ever have made. He said, "My father lives up yonder in that great big home. He has servants who are better off than I am. I am his son, but I'm living down here with the pigs. I will arise, and I will go to my father." No pig could say that, unless he was going in the opposite direction, heading back toward the pigpen.

Now what is the father going to do with his boy when he returns home? According to the Mosaic Law, that boy was to have been stoned to death (see Deut. 21:18–21)—but he wasn't stoned to death. The son went back and made his confession, "Father, I have sinned against heaven and against you." But his father wouldn't let him finish. You would expect the father to have said to one of his servants, "Go down and cut off some hickory limbs and bring them back to me. I'm going to whip this boy within an inch of his life. He has disgraced my name; he's spent my substance; he's wasted his time. He has been in sin, and I'm going to teach him." But that's not what happened at all. The boy, you see, had gotten his whipping in the far country. All prodigals get their whipping when they are away from home. When they come back to the heavenly Father, there is always a banquet, a robe, and a ring. And "they began to be merry." The fun was up at the father's house and never in the pigpen.

The interesting thing now is that Peter says, "And the sow that was washed [returned] to her wallowing in the mire." Now we can add something to the parable of the prodigal son. One of those little pigs in the pigpen said to the prodigal son, "You say you want to leave this lovely pigpen with all of this nice mud and goo, and you want to go up to your father's house? That sounds good; in fact, you've sold me. I think maybe I'd like to go up there with you and try it myself."

So the prodigal son told him, "If you go up there, things are sure going to be different! You are going to have to clean up."

When they got to the father's house, the father put his arms around the boy and said, "Bring forth the robe." Actually, he could smell those clothes his son had been wearing in the pigpen, and what he really meant was, "Give him a good bath and then put a new robe on him. He can't smell like that or live like that in my house."

The little pig went with the prodigal son, and he had to get all cleaned up too. They washed this little pig up nicely and tied a pink ribbon around his neck. They brushed his teeth with Pepsodent, and the little pig went squealing through the house. But it was only a couple of days until the little pig came to the prodigal son with a downcast look and said, "Prodigal Son, I don't like it here."

And the son said, "Why, I am having the best time I've ever had in my life since I came home, and you say you don't like it here! What's wrong?"

The little pig replied, "I don't like this idea of having white sheets on the bed. If we could just get to a place where there is plenty of good, sloppy mud, I could sleep better there."

"We just don't do that here in the father's house," said the prodigal son. "You just can't live in a pigpen here."

"Another thing I don't like is sitting at a table, using a knife and fork, and having a white tablecloth, and eating out of a plate. Why couldn't we have a trough down on the floor and put everything in there? We could all jump in and have the biggest time of our lives."

"We don't do that here?" said the son.

And the little pig said, "Well, I think I'll arise and go to my father." His old man wasn't in that house, and so he started back to his home. He had been all cleaned up, but he went back to the pigpen and found his old man right down in the middle of the biggest loblolly you've ever seen—mud all around him, dirty, filthy, and smelly. That little old pig began to squeal and made a leap for it. He jumped in right beside his father, saying, "Old man, I sure am glad to get back home!" You know why? Because he was a pig.

I had the privilege of being pastor in a downtown Los Angeles church beginning in 1949. Those were the years when subdivisions were beginning to be built in Southern California. That's the period when the population doubled again and again. People came from everywhere, and we saw a tremendous ingathering in the church I pastored during that period. I have always thanked the Lord that He gave me the privilege of being in that unique position at just the right time.

Although it was a great time because so many folk turned to the Lord, there was always the problem of how to tell the pigs from the sons—that is, professing Christians from real born-again believers. It was difficult and confusing, but I learned something. I found that at one end of the road was the Father's house, at the other end of the road was a pigpen, and there were always prodigal sons who were going back to the Father's house.

I talked to a preacher's son one time when he came in to see me. He was a handsome young man who had come out to Hollywood to make it big, but he was one of those who didn't have the charisma and didn't quite make it. He got in with the wrong crowd and began to drink. He saw that he was going down and down. He was a prodigal son—he wasn't a pig. He hated the life he had been living. When he came to see me, he said, "My dad is a wonderful man. I've let him down so, and I just don't know how he would receive me. I don't know whether I can go home or not."

I said, "Let me call him, and if he doesn't want to talk to you, we'll just hang up," and the boy agreed. So I called this man who is a very fine minister, and after we had exchanged a few pleasantries about the weather and such, I knew that he was wondering why I was calling him. I said, "I have somebody here in my study who would like to talk to you."

He knew who it was. He knew that his boy wasn't a pig but a son. That father broke down and said, "Is it my boy?"

I said, "Yes."

"Let me talk to him." The boy began to weep, and I'm sure the father was weeping too. I just walked out of my study to let them talk. I came back in after the young man had hung up, and he said to me, "I'm going home." However, the transition is always confusing because sometimes the prodigal sons are on the other side of the road going down to the pigpen. To add to the confusion, sometimes a pig will get out of the pigpen and go up to the Father's house. But he is a pig—he won't like it there. He may get all washed and cleaned up and become very religious. Sometimes he may even be made a deacon in the church. You just can't tell because he's all cleaned up on the outside; but inside he has the heart of a pig, and a pig loves the mire.

One time a lady came to me and said, "I used to know this man back East when he was a superintendent of a Sunday school and a deacon in the church. He's here on the West Coast now. He's drinking, he's divorced his wife, and he's running around. Is he saved or not?" I told her I didn't know, and she said, "You mean that you are a preacher and you don't know whether that man is saved or not?"

I said, "No, I really don't know. I couldn't tell you, because all I can see is the outside. But I'll tell you what we'll do. We are in this great metropolitan area where there is a road with a pigpen at one end of it and the Father's house at the other end. I've learned that, if you wait long enough, all the pigs will go down to the pigpen and all the prodigal sons will go home to the Father's house. Just wait and see. If that man continues to live in the pigpen, we can know that he is a pig—because Peter says that the pig that was washed has now returned to her wallowing in the mire."

This is the mark of the apostate, and it is a frightful picture. I know of no more frightful picture in the Word of God other than chapter 18 of the Book of Revelation.

I will conclude with a poem written by a friend who heard me preach on this subject of the prodigal pig.

A PIG IS A PIG

"Come home with me," said the prodigal son.
"We'll sing and dance and have lots of fun.

"We'll wine and dine with women and song.
You'll forget you're a pig before very long."

So the pig slipped out while the momma was asleep,
Shook off the mud from the mire so deep.

Around his neck was a bow so big,
He's gonna show the world, a pig's not a pig!

With his snout in the air he trotted along,
With the prodigal son who was singin' a song.

It must be great to be a rich man's son,
He would surely find out 'fore the day was done!

It didn't take him long to realize his mistake—
He'd been scrubbed and rubbed till his muscles ached!

He squealed when they put a gold ring in his nose
And winced with pain when they trimmed his toes.

He sat at the table on a stool so high,
A bib around his neck and a fork to try,

While the prodigal son, in his lovely robe,
Kept feeding his face, so glad to be home!

When the meat came around, the pig gave a moan—
It looked too much like a kind of his own.

He jumped from his chair with a grunt and a groan,
Darted through the door and headed for home.

His four little feet made the dust ride high
For he didn't stop till he reached that sty!

It's what's on the inside that counts, my friend,
For a pig is a pig to the very end!

                           —Evelyn C. Sanders

CHAPTER 3

THEME: Attitude toward return of the Lord, a test of
apostates; agenda of God for the world—past world,
present world, future world; admonition to believers

There are three major divisions in this chapter: (1) The attitude
toward the return to the Lord as a test of apostates; (2) the agenda
of God for the world; and (3) the admonition to believers.

This is another remarkable chapter which Peter has written.

ATTITUDE TOWARD RETURN OF THE LORD—
A TEST OF APOSTATES

**This second epistle, beloved, I now write unto you; in
both which I stir up your pure minds by way of remembrance [2 Pet. 3:1].**

Simon Peter makes it clear that he is the writer of both epistles.

"I stir up your pure minds"—"pure" is not the best translation. A
better translation would be "sincere." I don't think that the saints back
in Peter's day had minds which were any more pure than our minds
are today—and I haven't found anyone yet who I thought had a pure
mind. If you feel that you have a pure mind, I just haven't met you yet.

There is a certain cult which began in Chicago and majored in
contemplation. Instead of having a big temple, as many of the cults
do, this cult prepared little booths where a person may go and contemplate and think beautiful thoughts. These booths have beautiful
pictures in them; the furnishings are rather plush, and everything is
there for comfort to make the person *feel* good. Everything about the
surroundings is lovely. The person is to sit in that booth and think
pure thoughts.

I read about that when I was in Chicago many years ago and
thought I would try it out. I didn't want to go to the cult's booths; so I

sat in my hotel room. There were pictures on the wall—they weren't masterpieces, to be sure, but the room was attractive. I sat there and said to myself, "Now I am going to think some beautiful thoughts." Do you want to know something? I could think of the meanest, dirtiest things I have ever thought of in my whole life!

My friend, our minds are not pure minds, and the word Peter uses means "sincere" rather than pure. He is addressing genuine believers.

He is saying, "I want to stir up your sincere minds by *way of remembrance*." This is not something new he is going to talk to them about; he just wants to stir up their memories.

A man said to me, "I have a good memory. My problem is that my forgettery is even better." Well, many of us have that same problem, and Simon Peter could tell you about it from his own experience. On that night when he denied our Lord while he was warming his hands by the enemy's fire, he forgot all about the fact that the Lord Jesus had said that he would deny Him. The record tells us, "And the Lord turned, and looked upon Peter. And Peter remembered the word of the Lord, how he had said unto him, Before the cock crow, thou shalt deny me thrice" (Luke 22:61). Peter had forgotten all about it, you see. He had the same frailties that we have, and so he wants to stir up their (and our) sincere minds by way of remembrance.

Now what is it that he wants them to remember?

That ye may be mindful of the words which were spoken before by the holy prophets, and of the commandment of us the apostles of the Lord and Saviour [2 Pet. 3:2].

"The holy prophets" are the Old Testament writers. "And of the commandment of us the apostles." Notice that Simon Peter doesn't put himself in a position of being above the other apostles; he is just one of the boys. Before he finishes this epistle, he will refer to something Paul had written, which means he includes Paul as an apostle also. He is saying that the things he is going to remind them of had been written about by the other apostles and also had been the subject of the Old Testament prophets.

Now notice the subject—

Knowing this first, that there shall come in the last days scoffers, walking after their own lusts [2 Pet. 3:3].

"Knowing this first"—this was something they were to know first of all.

"There shall come in the last days"—these are the days in which you and I live, and they will continue on into the Great Tribulation period after the church is gone from the earth.

"Scoffers" will be the apostates whom he described so vividly back in chapter 2. These scoffers evidently will be members of churches, and many of them pastors, who will be "walking after their own lusts," their own desires, not attempting to follow the Word of God. You see, it is this type of person who attacks the truths of the Bible. If a man is willing to forsake his sins and is willing to receive Christ, God will make His Word real to him. Paul, writing in 2 Corinthians 3, said that a veil is over their minds; but if their hearts will turn to God, the veil will be removed. Their problem is not intellectual; their problem is heart trouble. And so they put forward a false argument:

And saying, Where is the promise of his coming? for since the fathers fell asleep, all things continue as they were from the beginning of the creation [2 Pet. 3:4].

"Where is the promise of his coming?" In other words, they will say something like this, "Some of you premillennial folk have been saying for years that the Lord Jesus is going to come back and take the church out of the world, and then after a seven-year period of tribulation, He will come to the earth to establish His Kingdom. Well, where is He? Why hasn't He come?" They are going to scoff at it. The second coming of Christ will be denied—not only by the atheist or Communist standing out yonder on a soap box, but it will also be denied by those who stand in the pulpit and profess to be believers.

Now what did the Old Testament prophets write about? They wrote about the coming of Christ to the earth to establish His Kingdom. What did the New Testament apostles write about? They wrote about Christ's coming to take the church out of the world and then, after the Great Tribulation, about His coming to the earth to establish His Kingdom. Notice that the Old Testament prophets did not write about the church—not one of them did. They wrote only about His coming to earth to establish His Kingdom.

It was the Lord Jesus Himself who first revealed that He would be coming for His own. He said, as recorded in John, ". . . I go to prepare a place for you. And if I go and prepare a place for you, I will come again, and receive you unto myself . . ." (John 14:2–3). The place He was going to prepare was not down here. It was not on the other side of the Mount of Olives—if you doubt that, go look at it; it is a desolate place. Our Lord went back to heaven, and that is where He is preparing a place for us. And He promised to come back for us. In 1 Thessalonians 4:17, we are told that we will meet Him in the air.

Let me repeat: The prophecy in the Old Testament of Christ's coming was to establish His Kingdom upon the earth; the prophecy in the New Testament of His coming was first to take His church out of the world and then to come to establish His Kingdom upon the earth.

"For since the fathers fell asleep, all things continue as they were from the beginning of the creation." This is the "proof" which the scoffers will offer, and, by the way, it is the most prevalent argument given in our day. "The fathers" would refer all the way back to father Adam.

The scoffers adopt the doctrine of *laissez faire* or let's continue with the status quo. Nothing unusual has happened in the past. Things have just progressed along. Man has evolved, and things have come along gently and nicely in the past. Peter is going to say, "That's where you are absolutely wrong. If you think nothing has happened in the past, let me tell you about it!"

AGENDA OF GOD FOR THE WORLD

Now Peter is going to talk about three worlds in one. That is not something strange to us. Older folk will remember using two-in-one shoe polish. Then there was a sewing machine company that put out three-in-one oil. Well, you and I live in a three-in-one world.

We have been hearing a great deal about one world, and certainly the world is moving toward the day when a world dictator will take over. I don't think there is any question about that in the minds of thoughtful men. Great thinkers of this century have taken the position that we have come to a crisis and to the end of man on the earth.

PAST WORLD

Peter presents a three-in-one world. Let's first look at world number one, the world that *was*.

> **For this they willingly are ignorant of, that by the word of God the heavens were of old, and the earth standing out of the water and in the water:**
>
> **Whereby the world that then was, being overflowed with water, perished [2 Pet. 3:5–6].**

"For this they *willingly* are ignorant of." My, this puts a great many scientists and Ph.D.'s in a pretty bad light!

"The world that then was, being overflowed with water, perished." That is, the world of people and of animals disappeared. This could refer to the world before Adam was put here, or it could refer to the Flood in Noah's day. I have vacillated between these two viewpoints, but I lean toward the latter now.

Regarding the first viewpoint, let me say that many of us believe that there is a hiatus between Genesis 1:1 and Genesis 1:2 and that a great catastrophe took place at that time. Today this view is largely rejected by the majority of Christians who are scientists. However, scientists change their theories over the years, and I am not prepared to go along with them yet.

There was a judgment in the pre-Adamic world, before man was put here. We have a suggestion of what took place in Isaiah 14:12–14: "How art thou fallen from heaven, O Lucifer, son of the morning! how art thou cut down to the ground, which didst weaken the nations! For thou hast said in thine heart, I will ascend into heaven, I will exalt my throne above the stars of God: I will sit also upon the mount of the congregation, in the sides of the north: I will ascend above the heights of the clouds; I will be like the most High." Satan's desire was never to be *unlike* God. He wanted to take God's place. And there are a great many human beings who want to be little gods down here. Any man who is working on his own salvation, whose theory is that he is good enough for heaven, ignores the fact that he is dealing with the holy God. He does not seem to realize that man is a sinner, that man is lost, and that God has provided a way of redemption for him. The Lord Jesus said, ". . . no man cometh unto the Father, but by me" (John 14:6). Remember that it was the God-man who said that! Now, if you think you can go to the Father on your own, what you are saying is this: "Move over, God. I'm coming up to sit beside you because I am a god also." That, you see, was Satan's desire, and it occasioned a judgment which evidently took out of heaven a great company of angels who had joined forces with Satan, Lucifer, son of the morning.

The other possibility is that Peter is speaking about the water judgment that took place in Noah's day. I have asked several outstanding Bible teachers what judgment they thought Peter had in mind, and there was some disagreement although most of them thought it referred to the Flood of Noah's day. Surely that seems to be the suggestion here.

The antediluvian civilization was destroyed with a flood, and there is abundant evidence for this. The great shaft which was put down at the site of ancient Ur of the Chaldees shows that there were several civilizations destroyed. In the excavation, the archaeologists came to a great deal of sand and silt with quite a bit of sediment which was deposited there by a flood. Then beneath all this, they found the remains of a very high civilization. Personally, I believe that Peter refers directly to the Flood of Noah's day, and surely this earth bears abundant evidence of such a flood.

Now, whether Peter was referring to the pre-Adamic judgment or to the judgment in Noah's day is a matter of conjecture. It makes no difference at all which view you hold as to *when* the world was "overflowed with water, [and] perished." The important thing is that it did occur at some point in the past. There is abundant evidence that some great cataclysm did take place and that all things have not continued as they were from the beginning of the creation.

PRESENT WORLD

Now Peter presents world number two, the world that *is*. You and I live in world number two.

> **But the heavens and the earth, which are now, by the same word are kept in store, reserved unto fire against the day of judgment and perdition of ungodly men [2 Pet. 3:7].**

This says that this earth has been stored up for fire. This is a very interesting expression, by the way, and it not only means stored up *for* fire but also stored up *with* fire (that could easily be the translation of it). The suggestion is that there are resident forces present in the world which could destroy it. It is not that God is going to rain fire down from heaven but that this earth carries its own judgment. How well we know this today! You and I are living on a powder keg—or, more literally, on an atom bomb. There will never be another flood to destroy the world. That judgment is past; water destroyed the world that *was*. Now the world that *is* is reserved for another judgment, the judgment of fire. In other words, this present order of things in this world is temporary. It is moving toward another judgment, and Peter will give us more details in verse 10.

"Kept in store" is the same Greek word that the Lord Jesus used when He told of the man who was laying up treasure. Well, God had been laying up this secret of how He made this universe, and it seems that man has broken into God's secret treasure house. It seems that man has opened a veritable Pandora's box, and today thoughtful men are frightened.

Dr. Urey from the University of Chicago, who worked on the atomic bomb, began an article several years ago in Collier's magazine by saying, "I am a frightened man, and I want to frighten you."

Winston Churchill said, "Time is short."

Mr. Luce, the owner of *Life, Time,* and *Fortune* magazines, addressed a group of missionaries who were the first to return to their fields after World War II. Speaking in San Francisco, he made the statement that when he was a boy, the son of a Presbyterian missionary in China, he and his father often discussed the premillennial coming of Christ, and he thought that all missionaries who believed in that teaching were inclined to be fanatical. And then Mr. Luce said, "I wonder if there wasn't something to that position after all."

Dr. Charles Beard, the American historian, says, "All over the world the thinkers and searchers who scan the horizon of the future are attempting to assess the values of civilization and speculating about its destiny."

Dr. William Yogt, in the *Road to Civilization*, said, "The handwriting on the wall of five continents now tells us that the Day of Judgment is at hand."

Dr. Raymond B. Fosdick, president of the Rockefeller Foundation, said, "To many ears comes the sound of the tramp of doom. Time is short."

H. G. Wells declared before he died, "This world is at the end of its tether. The end of everything we call life is close at hand."

General Douglas MacArthur said, "We have had our last chance."

Former President Dwight Eisenhower said, "Without a moral regeneration throughout the world there is no hope for us as we are going to disappear one day in the dust of an Atomic Explosion."

And Dr. Nicholas Murray Butler, ex-president of Columbia University, said, "The end cannot be far distant."

If men from all walks of life are speaking in this manner, certainly you and I, who have believed the Bible and who have had through all these years such a clear statement concerning the judgment that is coming upon this world and the way in which it is to be destroyed, should be alert. Do not misunderstand me, I am not saying that the atomic bomb will be God's method for the destruction of this world. I am merely saying that man at last has found out that this passage in 2 Peter makes good sense. This is a way that is not only logical but is scientific by which God can destroy this universe.

But, beloved, be not ignorant of this one thing, that one day is with the Lord as a thousand years, and a thousand years as one day [2 Pet. 3:8].

Now it is obvious that the destruction of the earth and heavens will take place during the Day of the Lord, which is an extended period of time including the seven years of tribulation and the one thousand years of the millennial Kingdom. When the Lord Jesus returns to the earth at the end of the Great Tribulation period and establishes His Kingdom here, He is going to renovate this earth—but that will not be a permanent renovation. Not until after the Tribulation and after the Millennium will the dissolution of the earth and the heavens (of which Peter speaks) occur. So you see, my friend, even if the Rapture should take place tomorrow, it still would be a thousand and seven years before this destruction.

The Lord is not slack concerning his promise, as some men count slackness; but is longsuffering to us-ward, not willing that any should perish, but that all should come to repentance [2 Pet. 3:9].

God is long-suffering; He is patient; He is not rushing things. After all, He has eternity behind Him and eternity ahead of Him. He doesn't need to worry about time! To Him a thousand years is as one day and one day is as a thousand years. But the point is that the final judgment, the dissolution of the earth and the heavens, is coming. In the meantime, He is giving men everywhere a further opportunity to repent and turn to Himself. This is the reason you and I need to get the Word of God out. It is the only thing that can change hearts and lives. It is by the Word of God that folk are born again—as Peter said in his first epistle, "Being born again, not of corruptible seed, but of incorruptible, by the word of God, which liveth and abideth for ever" (1 Pet. 1:23).

"Not willing that any should perish, but that all should come to repentance." It is not God's will that you should perish. One of the reasons that you have been reading this book is simply because God does not want you to come into judgment; He wants you to pass from death unto life. And you can do that—you can turn to Him and receive the wonderful salvation that He has for you.

Do you know that you cannot keep God from loving you? You can reject His love, but you cannot keep Him from loving you. Neither can you keep it from raining, but you can raise an umbrella to keep the rain from falling on you. Also, you can raise the umbrella of indifference or the umbrella of sin or the umbrella of rebellion so that you won't experience God's love, but you cannot keep Him from loving you.

A story comes out of Greek mythology which illustrates my point: A young man had a very wonderful mother, but he fell in love with a very ungodly girl. The ungodly girl hated the boy's mother and could not bear to be in her presence. It was not because the mother rebuked her, but her very character and her very presence were a rebuke to this girl. Nevertheless, this boy was desperately in love with her, for she was beautiful. And finally he pleaded with her to marry him, and she said, "Only on one condition: you must cut out your mother's heart and bring it to me." Well, this boy was so madly in love and so desperate that he descended to the low plane of committing this diabolical deed. He killed his mother, cut out her heart and was taking it to the girl when, on the way, he stumbled and fell. The heart spoke out, "My son, did you hurt yourself?"

My friend, you can slap God in the face; you can turn your back on Him; you can blaspheme Him, but you cannot keep Him from wanting to save you. You cannot keep Him from loving you, for He provided a Savior, His own Son, to die in your place. The Lord Jesus will save you if you will receive the salvation He offers. My friend, things are not going to continue as they are now. Oh, I know the monotony of life today, the ennui of it all. Well, it is coming to an end, and judgment *will* come. You and I are living in a world which is moving toward judgment.

But the day of the Lord will come as a thief in the night; in the which the heavens shall pass away with a great noise, and the elements shall melt with fervent heat, the

earth also and the works that are therein shall be burned up [2 Pet. 3:10].

"But the day of the Lord will come as a thief in the night." There is some argument as to whether this takes place at the coming of Christ to establish His Kingdom or at the end of the millennial Kingdom. I am convinced that the Day of the Lord is an extended period of time which opens with the Tribulation, followed by the thousand-year reign of Christ, the brief rebellion led by Satan, and the judgment of the Great White Throne. Then, as we find in the Book of Revelation, the new heavens and the new earth come into view.

"As a thief in the night," the same expression which Paul uses in 1 Thessalonians 5:2, indicates that it will begin unexpectedly.

"In the which the heavens shall pass away with a great noise." The Greek word used here for "noise" is rhoizēdon. It is the word used for the swish of an arrow, the rush of wings, the splash of water, the hiss of a serpent. Have you ever listened to an atom bomb go off? Do you remember a number of years ago when they were experimenting with the bombs and we could see and hear them on television? This is the very word and the only word I know that could describe such a noise.

"And the elements shall melt with fervent heat." You see, matter is not eternal as was once believed; you can get rid of matter—that is, it can be converted into energy. Peter speaks here of "the elements," the little building blocks of the universe, the stoicheia as it is in the Greek. Stoicheion is a better word than our word atom which comes from a Greek word meaning something you cannot cut, because we have found that an atom can be cut and it can be taken apart.

"Melt" employs one of the simplest Greek words, the verb luō, which simply means "to untie or to unloose." By untying the atom, man has been able to produce a little bomb that can do tremendous wonders. Today men are trying to release that energy because you and I live in a world that is running out of resources. When God stocked this earth, He put plenty of oil in it, and He put plenty of groceries here. It was like a great supermarket. Men came and prostituted this earth. They have polluted the earth and are beginning to use up all that God had put in the pantry and all that He had put in the filling station. But there is a tremendous potential of energy in the little atom, and I tell you, when God destroys this earth someday, it is going to be a tremendous thing. I think that it will be just like a great atomic explosion, and the earth will go into nothing. I have always felt that the Lord will probably turn the little atoms wrong side out and use the other side of them for a while. When He does that, man will never be able to untie them again.

"The earth also and the works that are therein shall be burned up." This will certainly include the tremendous amount of water that is on the earth—it will be burned up. We know today that water is made up of two elements, hydrogen and oxygen, and both of them are gases that are inflammable and can be very explosive. Firemen tell us that there are certain kinds of fire which, when water is put on them, are only helped along by it. Firefighters have to use certain kinds of chemicals to put out such fires. "The works that are therein shall be burned up."

Peter is saying that God will judge in the future just as He has in the past. At the beginning of this chapter, Peter says that the scoffers will say, "All things continue as they were from the beginning of the creation" (v. 4). The scoffer's great fallacy is in not knowing the past, yet it is the evolutionist who makes so much of the fact that there was a great catastrophe in the past. The great mountains out here in the West, the High Sierras, were thrown up at that time by some great convulsion of nature. That happened sometime in the past, and it was a judgment of God, if you please.

The Day of the Lord will include judgment also. The "day of the Lord" is a familiar term in Scripture. The prophets used it, the Lord Jesus used it, and many of the New Testament writers used it. It is a technical term. The Day of the Lord begins in darkness, as the Old Testament prophets said—it begins with tribulation. It ends with this great atomic explosion, this great judgment of the earth by its being dissolved by fire. Between these two great events is the period of the seven years of tribulation, the coming of Christ to the earth to establish His Kingdom, the millennial Kingdom, the brief release of Satan and the rebellion of those who rally to him, Satan's final confinement, and the Great White Throne judgment of the lost. Then after the judgment of the earth, which Peter is describing, the new heaven and the new earth come into view.

> **Seeing then that all these things shall be dissolved, what manner of persons ought ye to be in all holy conversation and godliness [2 Pet. 3:11].**

Now Peter says that, in view of the fact of what has happened and what God is going to do in the future, you and I ought not to be standing on the sidelines, twiddling our thumbs, and indulging in criticism. Christians find it so easy to criticize others, but specifically, what are you doing today to get out the Word of God? That is the important question in this hour for every Christian, every church, every pastor. Every person sitting in the pew needs to say to himself: "I am not here to sit in judgment on the preacher; I'm not here to judge other Christians; I am here to get out the Word of God, to do something positive. The question is: What am I doing to that end?"

> **Looking for and hasting unto the coming of the day of God, wherein the heavens being on fire shall be dissolved, and the elements shall melt with fervent heat? [2 Pet. 3:12].**

"Looking for and hasting unto the coming of the day of God." Peter is writing to the *Diaspora*, the Jews scattered abroad, and he says that the day of God is coming.

"Wherein the heavens being on fire shall be dissolved." After the dissolution of the present heavens, the day of God, which is eternity, as we see in Revelation 21:1, will come.

"Wherein the heavens being on fire shall be dissolved, and the elements shall melt with fervent heat?" This is one of the most remarkable statements you could possibly have coming from a fisherman on the Sea of Galilee. I don't imagine that Peter figured out how the water, that sea where he fished, would burn. He didn't know how all this could be dissolved and melted. But the elements, that which we call atoms, the building blocks of the universe, are to be absolutely melted. However, this time Peter uses a different Greek word for "melt" than he used in verse 10. It is *tēkomai*, a word that means actually "wasting away, the wasting away of nature." This could possibly suggest the effects of radioactivity when an atomic bomb goes off.

FUTURE WORLD

Now Peter comes to that which is ahead—the world that *shall* be. Just because the earth will be dissolved does not mean that God is through with the earth. As the earth was judged in the past, it will be judged in the future, but the earth will go on.

Nevertheless we, according to his promise, look for new heavens and a new earth, wherein dwelleth righteousness [2 Pet. 3:13].

Righteousness does not *dwell* in this earth today. It is not at home in this earth. It's not at home in Washington, D.C. It's not at home in any of the capitals of the world. It's not at home in your hometown, and it's not at home where you live today. But righteousness will dwell in the new earth and in the new heavens.

In *Hamlet* Shakespeare described his day by saying, "The times *are* out of joint." He was right—the times *are* out of joint. Some other poets have waxed rather eloquent, have soared to the heights and, I think, have misrepresented things. For instance, Browning, in "Pippa Passes," wrote:

> The lark's on the wing;
> The snail's on the thorn:
> God's in his heaven—
> All's right with the world!

The lark is on the wing, the snail is on the thorn (in fact, he's in my backyard), God *is* in His heaven, but things are *not* right in the world today. I'm glad there is another world, a new heaven and a new earth, that is coming on. It is going to be wonderful. I have always enjoyed trading in my old car and getting a new model. God has a new model of the earth coming on, and I'll be glad when it arrives. It will be a wonderful earth because it will be characterized by righteousness, and it will be an earth in which righteousness will actually *dwell*.

ADMONITION TO BELIEVERS

Wherefore, beloved, seeing that ye look for such things, be diligent that ye may be found of him in peace, without spot, and blameless [2 Pet. 3:14].

"Wherefore, beloved, seeing that ye look for such things"—that is, since we know that the earth and all its works will be burned up, we realize how important a life of godliness is here and now. We are to live a holy life down here, a life separated unto God. Friend, after all, what is really worthwhile in this earth today? What are your goals? Are you a productive Christian moving toward a worthwhile goal? Somebody says, "I want to raise my family." That's worthwhile. Somebody else says, "I want to make a good living for my family and to educate my children." That's worthwhile. Although these things are worthwhile, what is really the object of your life? Is it to live for God? If you live for God, all of these secondary issues, I believe, will take care of themselves.

And account that the longsuffering of our Lord is salvation; even as our beloved brother Paul also according to the wisdom given unto him hath written unto you [2 Pet. 3:15].

"The longsuffering of our Lord is salvation." That is, His patience in delaying His return in judgment is providing an opportunity for men to be saved. Our patient waiting is a mental adjustment to the present world situation. We do not need to be alarmed today. God is in His heaven. Things are not right in the world, but He is going to make them right someday. This is the message of the New Testament, and Peter reminds us that Paul also wrote of this.

> **As also in all his epistles, speaking in them of these things; in which are some things hard to be understood, which they that are unlearned and unstable wrest, as they do also the other scriptures, unto their own destruction [2 Pet. 3:16].**

Peter says that what Paul wrote was Scripture. And he says that Paul wrote of truth in depth. He certainly did that, and in my opinion Peter did that pretty well himself here in this epistle.

> **Ye therefore, beloved, seeing ye know these things before, beware lest ye also, being led away with the error of the wicked, fall from your own stedfastness [2 Pet. 3:17].**

There is something that we are to *know*, my friend. Oh, don't be a lazy Christian not learning the Word of God. There is no little gimmick, there is no little course you can take in a week, there is no little program that you can go through that will change and revolutionize your life—there is no easy way. We are to seriously study the entire Word of God, not just a few little verses of Scripture that we throw about and kick around like a football. Peter says, "Ye know these things before, beware lest ye also, being led away with the error of the wicked, fall from your own stedfastness." My friend, if you have a comprehensive knowledge of Scripture and apply it to your own life, you will be a steadfast Christian.

As we saw at the beginning of this epistle, Peter's characteristic word is *knowledge*. The epitome of his entire epistle is expressed in the injunction of this final verse:

> **But grow in grace, and in the knowledge of our Lord and Saviour Jesus Christ. To him be glory both now and for ever. Amen [2 Pet. 3:18].**

"Grow in grace and in the knowledge of our Lord and Saviour Jesus Christ." True knowledge is not some esoteric information concerning a form or formula, a rite or ritual; nor is it some secret order or password, as the Gnostics claimed. It is to know Jesus Christ as He is revealed to man in the Word of God. This is the secret of life and of Christian living (see John 17:3).

Notice how Peter uses the name—"our Lord and Saviour Jesus Christ." How precious the Lord Jesus had become to this rough, old fisherman! As J. Niebor has well said, "He obeyed Him as Lord, he loved Him as Saviour, he adored Him as the greatest human, Jesus, he worshipped Him as the mighty anointed Son of God, Christ."

Peter concludes his swan song with this paean of praise: "To him be glory both now and for ever. Amen."

Oh, my friend, that you and I might *know* Jesus Christ! Someone has put it like this:

> We mutter and sputter;
> We fume and we spurt;
> We mumble and grumble;
> Our feelings get hurt.
>
> We can't understand things;
> Our vision grows dim,
> When all that we need
> Is a moment with Him.
> —Author unknown

Only as we spend time with Him, as He is revealed in His Word, can we grow in our knowledge of Him.

BIBLIOGRAPHY

(Recommended for Further Study)

Barbieri, Louis A. *First and Second Peter*. Chicago, Illinois: Moody Press, 1977. (A fine, inexpensive survey.)

Criswell, W. A. *Expository Sermons on the Epistles of Peter*. Grand Rapids, Michigan: Zondervan Publishing House, 1976.

English, E. Schuyler. *The Life and Letters of St. Peter*. New York, New York: Our Hope, 1941. (Excellent.)

Ironside, H. A. *Notes on James and Peter*. Neptune, New Jersey: Loizeaux Brothers, n.d.

Kelly, William. *The Epistles of Peter*. Addison, Illinois: Bible Truth Publishers, n.d.

Robertson, A. T. *Epochs in the Life of Simon Peter*. Grand Rapids, Michigan: Baker Book House, 1933.

Thomas, W. H. Griffith. *The Apostle Peter*. Grand Rapids, Michigan: Wm. B. Eerdmans Publishing Co., 1956. (Excellent.)

Wolston, W. T. P. *Simon Peter—His Life and Letters*. 1896 reprint. Addison, Illinois: Bible Truth Publishers, n.d. (Excellent.)

Wuest, Kenneth S. *In These Last Days*. Grand Rapids, Michigan: Wm. B. Eerdmans Publishing Co., 1954. (Deals with the Epistles of 2 Peter, John, and Jude.)